How to
Teach EAL
Students
in the
Classroom
The Complete Guide

Mike Gershon

1400 Centrepark Blvd., Ste 1000
West Palm Beach, FL 33401
717.845.6300
email: pub@learningsciences.com
learningsciences.com

Printed in the United States of America

22   21   20   19   18   1   2   3   4   5

Names: Gershon, Mike, author.

Title: How to teach EAL students in the classroom : the complete guide / Mike Gershon.

Description: West Palm Beach, FL : Learning Sciences, 2018. | Series: Great teaching made easy. | Previously released in the UK in 2013 by Mike Gershon.

Identifiers: LCCN 2018945744 | ISBN 978-1-943920-43-3 (pbk.) | ISBN 978-1-943920-44-0 (ebook)

Subjects: LCSH: English language--Study and teaching--Foreign speakers. | Second language acquisition--Study and teaching. | Language and languages--Study and teaching. | Student growth (Academic achievement) | Effective teaching. | BISAC: EDUCATION / Teaching Methods & Materials / Language Arts. | EDUCATION / Multicultural Education. | EDUCATION / Professional Development.

Classification: LCC PE1128.A2 G47 2018 (print) | LCC PE1128.A2 (ebook) | DDC 428.0071--dc23.

Series Introduction

The 'How to…' series developed out of Mike Gershon's desire to share great classroom practice with teachers around the world. He wanted to put together a collection of books which would help professionals no matter what age group or subject they were teaching.

Each volume focuses on a different element of classroom practice, and each is overflowing with brilliant, practical strategies, techniques, and activities – all of which are clearly explained and ready-to-use. In most cases, the ideas can be applied immediately, helping teachers not only to teach better but to save time as well.

All of the books have been designed to help teachers. Each one goes out of its way to make educators' lives easier and their lessons even more engaging, inspiring, and successful than they already are.

In addition, the whole series is written from the perspective of a working teacher. It takes account of the realities of the classroom, blending theoretical insight with a relentlessly practical focus.

The 'How to…' series is great teaching made easy.

Author Introduction

Mike Gershon is a teacher, trainer, and writer. He is the author of over forty books on teaching, learning, and education, including a number of bestsellers, as well as the coauthor of four others. Mike's online resources have been viewed and downloaded more than 3.5 million times by teachers in over 180 countries and territories. He writes for the *Times Educational Supplement* and has created over eighty guides to different areas of teaching and learning as well as two online courses covering outstanding teaching and growth mindsets. Find out more, get in touch, and download free resources at www.mikegershon.com or www.learning sciences.com/mikegershon.

Acknowledgments

First and foremost I must thank Jeremy Hayward, who taught me to teach. He has been a major influence, and he is, without doubt, the best teacher I know. Thanks also to the many great teachers I have had over the years, specifically Judith Schofield, Richard Murgatroyd, Simon Mason, Cath Nealon, Andrew Gilliland, Graham Ferguson, and Simon Ditchfield. I must also thank all the wonderful teachers I have worked with and learnt from at Central Foundation Girls' School; Nower Hill High School; Pimlico Academy; and King Edward VI School, Bury St. Edmunds. Special mention must go to the Social Sciences team at Pimlico, to Jon Mason, and to James Wright. Of course, I cannot fail to thank all the fantastic students I have had the pleasure of teaching – particularly all the members of HC and HD at Pimlico. In addition, I am greatly indebted to the people I trained with at the IOE and, in particular, to Erin, Liam, Anna, and Rahwa. Finally, thanks to my mum for her unfailing support over the years and her wonderful example.

I have picked up many of the activities, strategies, and techniques in this book from the countless wonderful people I have worked with; however, any errors or omissions remain my own.

Table of Contents

CHAPTER ONE

Introduction

The Book

Welcome to *How to Teach EAL Students in the Classroom*. This book is your one-stop reference point for working with English as an additional language (EAL) learners. It has been designed with whole-class teaching in mind, but it can be adapted to suit one-on-one and small-group teaching as well.

I have divided the book into four sections, each focussing on a certain theme. This means that strategies, activities, and techniques are grouped into smaller collections, making the book easier to navigate. I have provided a rationale and explanation for each section.

The book contains a wide range of classroom tools which you can take and use immediately with little or no alteration. That said, nothing in here is set in stone, and you can easily adapt the contents to suit your needs, the needs of your pupils, or your style of teaching.

Suffice to say though, if like many of us there is a high premium on your time, the resources contained in the following pages will allow you to support your EAL learners quickly and effectively, whatever the lesson. You could pick nearly any strategy in here, go into your classroom tomorrow morning, and start using it without any further ado.

Thinking Carefully about Learners and Language

When working with EAL learners it is worth remembering these three words: Eyes, Speech, Body. They provide a simple means by which to consider the experience of the EAL learner in the classroom. By keeping them in mind, you can continually check whether what is happening is helping students or hindering them.

Ask yourself whether what the EAL learner can *see* will help them access and understand what is going on.

Ask whether what they can *hear* is helping them understand what is going on and what is expected of them.

Ask if you are using *your body* to support your spoken communication. Are you mirroring or supplementing the meaning of the words you are using? Are you remaining open? Are you physically modelling ideas? And are you modelling what it is that you want students to do?

Referring to these key words – using them as lenses – also causes the teacher to sympathise with the position of the EAL learner. It encourages them to view what is going on in the classroom from the perspective of someone for whom the main mode of expression is not fully accessible. This may sound obvious, yet it is easy to lose sight of such an important point amid the clamour for attention made by students, colleagues, and parents.

The following section looks at language and the experience of EAL learners in more detail. It also reflects on the role of the teacher in the classroom and thinks about student-teacher relationships. General suggestions are offered which supplement the specific activities and strategies explained in the rest of the book.

Praise, Emotion, and Individual Differences

Students who have English as an additional language (EAL) are, in many ways, no different from the rest of your students. They are still young people, they still have feelings, they still desire to do well, and they still have family or carers whom they go home to every night. As such, like everyone else, they will respond well to sympathy and praise, although any hint of a patronising manner must be avoided.

Sympathy should be used to indicate the teacher's understanding of the game – the knowledge of what is at issue for the learner and how they and the teacher are working together to try to overcome it: sympathy as shared understanding rather than tea and biscuits.

Praise must also be given out with care and thought. Never scrimp on it; do not treat it as a limited resource. Do be mindful, however, of the potential that exists for diluting its impact. There can be a temptation to praise a student who has English as an additional language for myriad minor things. The hope is that this will dissipate any anxiety or frustration they might be feeling due to their difficulties with communication. The learner may view this as patronising, though, or they may dislike the extra attention they are receiving.

Identify specific things for which to give praise, and make it clear to the learner (with gestures and modelling if necessary) precisely what it is you are praising. Such an approach smacks of honesty. It is difficult to see it as being anything other because it shows a clear thought process on behalf of the teacher. The approbation is directly tied to something the student has done, with an explanation as to why it is good. An argument is being advanced, with evidence to support it.

Emotion can play a significant role in any classroom. Managing it is a key part of ensuring good progress among learners and an atmosphere in which all feel safe and secure.

There are two things to say about emotion and EAL learners. The first is that one ought to expect periods of frustration, annoyance, or irritation. Anybody who finds themself in a situation where the expectations are unclear or it is not apparent what one is supposed to be doing can feel awkward and ill at ease. If the situation continues, these feelings can grow. I can recall losing my cool when someone who I was interviewing continually evaded the questions: it was frustrating to feel my own language being disempowered. Whilst this situation is not identical to that of an EAL learner, it still points to how disruption or dissonance in communication can draw out negative feelings.

In addition to this, it is important to remember that learning an additional language is, for most people, hard. Consider that an EAL learner is doing it 'on-the-go' and may have few (if any) native speakers around them, and one can see a hard task getting harder and harder. What is more, frustration can be made worse by students' difficulties in communicating their feelings to peers or to the teacher.

One of the fundamental facets of language is that it allows us to make others aware of our internal states. Knowing how to do this in one's first language yet not being able to do it in an additional language can be deeply frustrating. It is as if a barrier has been erected and one's own self has had to withdraw from the surroundings. Sharing our internal states helps us say who we are and signal our existence to others, as well as our independence. So, after all that is temporarily taken away, do not be surprised if EAL learners display some negative emotions at times!

The second point regarding emotion concerns the teacher. We are all used to communicating seemingly at will with our classes. We modify our language so as to ensure everyone follows what is being taught, but we work from a premise that simple alterations are all that is required to guarantee understanding. This comes from the fact that we know our students are versed in the English language. We know as well that a major part of our job is to continually develop and refine that understanding, but this begins from a vast shared pool of vocabulary, syntax, and grammar.

Working with EAL learners can be frustrating for the teacher. It can cause them to feel inept or powerless in the face of what sometimes appear to be insurmountable barriers. If one is used to providing help and support for learners, the loss of this ability can be difficult to deal with. It is easy to feel disoriented or helpless when all the tools which we would usually use to assist a child are no longer any good (or, at least, not as good as they would usually be).

If you find yourself in such a situation, I advise taking a three-pronged approach. First, do not despair. The decreased efficacy of your usual tools and techniques is not a reflection on you or the student.

Second, use this knowledge to imaginatively draw yourself and the student together. Acknowledge that the issue (not the problem) is for both of you and that it exists separately to the pair of you. By doing this, one avoids tying emotions to the issue. Also, you will create an external focal point which you and the student can bond over. It is akin to saying: 'At present we cannot communicate that well with each other. Let's work as a team to overcome this.' Such a mind-set may be impossible to express explicitly to the student, but holding on to it and letting it inform your behaviour ought to be enough.

The third point is to build activities and strategies from this book (or elsewhere, or ones you think up yourself) into your teaching. Doing this means you are being positive and proactive. You are working from the premise that the issue is transitory and that it can and will be overcome. You are doing your duty as a professional and as a person. You are helping your student(s) and need not accept any feelings of frustration, powerlessness, or anxiety which may creep up on you.

It is worth remembering that learning a new language can take a while. Do not expect dramatic changes or overnight successes. In rare cases these may come, but in general the student's development will be gradual. They will be feeling their way into the language, testing out its possibilities, trialling the meanings of words and identifying how far they can be pushed and in what circumstances.

If, at some point in your life, you have learnt a new language, reflect on that experience. Ask yourself how you made progress and what sort of timescales accorded with your increasing mastery. It may be that you too found the process difficult. If this is the case, do not remember it and then stop. It may be useful for sympathising with an EAL learner, but what would be better would be for you to analyse why you found it difficult and to learn from this. You may find that your own experience provides you with pointers on how to adapt your classroom or your teaching.

Individual differences will play a part as well. As we said before, EAL learners are just like the rest of your students in many respects. This includes the varying cognitive abilities, prior schooling, and life experiences they bring with them. While the inability to communicate in a given language will most likely mask the true cognitive capabilities of a student, it can still be assumed that any population of EAL learners will include a range of abilities. This will have consequences for the speed at which pupils pick up English.

So too will the motivation students possess. It is often worth speaking to pastoral leaders (or, if your school has one, an EAL coordinator) to find out a little about the backgrounds of your EAL learners. There are many reasons why a family, or in some cases an individual child, may move to live in another country. These could range from the highly desirous – a parent is promoted to a prestigious head office position in an English-speaking city – to the truly awful – a family is forced to flee its country of origin so as to escape persecution during a civil war. Even within these two situations there is room for variation. A child in the first case may have no interest in their parent's good fortune and wish only to stay with their friends. A child in the second case might be relieved to be living in a safe country, even if the uprooting was beyond their control.

Each EAL student who you encounter will be different. Try to find out a little about their backgrounds so you can understand where they are coming from (literally and metaphorically). This will help you to help them. Be sure to assimilate the information they provide during lessons: how they interact with others, the personality they project, the manner in which they respond to you, how they appear to apply themselves in an unfamiliar environment. Build up a picture of them and use it to aid your teaching. Do be prepared for it to alter though. As students become more confident in the language of the classroom, so their personalities might change. Your assumptions, whether made unwittingly or not, may well be challenged.

Much of what I have said so far has presumed that EAL learners are homogenous in their relationship to English, if not in other areas. They come to learn it as an additional language, their development progresses and, finally, they master it.

This is true in a general sense. It is logically sound to assume the following: First, a person comes into contact with something they did not previously know. Second, they spend a period of time engaging with and experiencing that thing. Third, providing they persist in the process, they eventually become capable of using the thing on their own terms. This is a rough, overarching model for learning.

Yet, when we are teaching, we will not by necessity encounter EAL learners in this way. They will arrive in our classrooms already at a point in the process. Consider the following shape: a long, thin, double-end-ed arrow; a continuum. At one end are learners who are encountering English for the first time, at the other end are learners who are highly skilled in every aspect of the language.

We could place all of our students, whether they are EAL learners or not, on this continuum. In fact, we could place everyone we know on it. We could stretch it further and include a whole range of criteria by which to determine where precisely different individuals fit.

Its use for us, though, is simpler. Conceive of your EAL students as being on the continuum. Once you have spent some time teaching them, look to place them in your mind roughly where you think they are at. The more experience you have, the more accurate these judgements will become.

Most schools will assess EAL learners and indicate to which of the EAL stages their present abilities correlate. These are nationally agreed criteria, each one of which tallies with certain skills and abilities. It will be useful for you to get hold of this information, but I would counsel against using it in favour of your own judgements. See it as a supplement instead.

The advantage of the continuum approach is that it provides you with a mental model that is continuous rather than discrete. The EAL stages are discrete because a continuum would be unwieldy at national level. It would also rely on subjective judgements and therefore lose its standardising capacity.

So, take note of the EAL stages and familiarise yourself with what each one refers to, but do not write off your own judgement in favour of them. Remember that you spend five days a week with students and are constantly assessing their abilities, including the extent to which they are able to manipulate language. Call on these skills when working with EAL learners.

Assume that when they first arrive in your lesson they will be at some point on the continuum. Find out what EAL stage they are at and any extra information which is available and may be of help. Make a judgement. Be prepared to alter this judgement as you spend more time with them. Your interactions will alter accordingly. Initially, you may judge student A to be further along the continuum than student B. As such, you will use more developed language when speaking to student A. Given a couple of months, student B might have caught up, while student A has plateaued. You will refine your judgements and adjust your use of language accordingly.

Thinking with the continuum model is also helpful because it allows you to see EAL learners in relation to native speakers. It encompasses all students in the class and so avoids putting EAL students to one side as a separate and distinct group. It promotes equality while recognising that learners have different needs. It also signals the potential for using native speakers to help new language learners develop their communication skills.

The Four Elements of Language: Speaking, Listening, Reading, and Writing

Let us now think about the four elements which go to make up the English language: speaking, listening, reading, and writing.

While all of these share similarities, including certain prerequisites that lead to success, they are nonetheless different. Here are some activities you might like to try which make this point clearer:

- Have a conversation with a friend. Go away afterwards and write a short piece about the same topic. Observe what is lost and what is gained through writing.
- Listen to a play on the radio. Get hold of the script and read it yourself. Consider how these two experiences differ.
- Hold a discussion with your class concerning an interesting question. After, ask them to write an answer to the same question. Compare these. (It would be fruitful to make an audio recording of the discussion and make a direct comparison.)
- Pick a topic at random from the dictionary and write about it, without stopping, for two minutes. Read what you have written. Ask yourself whether it makes sense, if someone else would understand it, and how the act of reading it compares to the act of writing it.

The four elements of language make different requirements and have different effects.

Listening

Listening comes first. Babies can listen before they can speak. It is through listening that they learn language. The same is true of older children and adults. Many of the most effective language training programmes are centred on listening to native speakers and trying to imitate the sounds which they make. This is because, of course, any language is initially *just* sounds. Meaning is attached to the sounds, but we must learn this meaning as well.

When children are developing speech, they can physically indicate things they want by, for example, pointing or grabbing. Therefore, they know in some sense that these things are there, and they believe they have the capacity to interact with them (a baby *could* reach for a rainbow). These things, and let us take an example of a toy bus, have no linguistic meaning for the child as yet though. The child does not think 'I want the toy bus.' It sees something, yes, and it wants that thing, yes, but beyond this there is nothing to say.

As the child grows it comes to be aware of the particular sounds which parents and carers attach to the toy bus. This happens through the child listening. The attachments are arbitrary – a bus could be called a boogly-gloop – and so must be learnt. They are not innate to either the object or to the human species.

Think back to the first time you heard a piece of music which you immediately fell in love with. The chances are that, having listened to it again and again, you now hear it with great acuity. You can pick out key changes, the arrival of new instruments, and the modulations in the singer's voice (if there is a singer). It is unlikely you understood the song in this manner when you first heard it. Repeated listens have helped you to remember the song. This, in turn, has provided you with the capacity to analyse it. When you first heard it, it was all new. You were taking everything in. Your brain was immersed.

Listening, as such, can develop. The more familiar one becomes with sounds, the more one is able to deal actively with those sounds. This includes identifying the meaning which is attached to them. It also includes 'reading' the intonation with which they are said. 'Stop!' can carry many different meanings, all of which are dependent on the stress, pace, volume, and tone of the delivery.

Speaking

While listening comes first, it is not long followed by speaking, and, once that arrives, the two remain inseparable.

As you learn to speak a language you are able to communicate with others in an increasingly sophisticated way. The subject of this communication is either external or internal to the person in question. The former refers to things which exist beyond the individual, for example, a chair, a curtain, or another person. The latter refers to things which are inherent to the individual. These include feelings, opinions, beliefs, and so forth.

Mastering the basics of speech is vital if one is to become part of the social world. This is not to say those who cannot speak are outside of society. Clearly people use sign language to communicate, and even those with severe disabilities are able to convey some or many of their thoughts through alternative systems (which could include technological assistance in the form of computers).

Speaking, though, is the primary means humans have to share what is inside their heads. It is closely linked to the formation and maintenance of relationships. 'We don't speak anymore.' 'I can't communicate with him'. 'There has been an irreparable breakdown in communications.' These phrases apply in many situations involving two or more individuals. All indicate the absolute centrality of speech to human relationships.

The couple who 'don't speak anymore' are unlikely to remain together. The mother who 'can't communicate with' her teenage child is likely to feel like there is a gap developing between them. The warring factions who have 'an irreparable breakdown in communications' veer away from conciliation and mutual understanding and head towards animosity and suspicion.

Speaking, combined with listening, is the mainstay of language. It is the natural, nurtured component which provides for our innate need to bond with one another and the skill, however first developed, to learn and to pass on information about ourselves and the world.

Returning briefly to the issue of emotion, the temporary inability to make their thoughts understood can be deeply frustrating for EAL learners (so too for the teacher). Equally, the teacher's knowledge that the efficacy of their own speech is limited (or, in some cases, nil) – because upon hearing it the learner does not understand it – is also frustrating. The learner may feel the same. They hear what seems to be an undifferentiated, meaningless mass of sounds, yet they know there must be some meaning hidden within, if only they had the means by which to access it.

Speaking and listening account for much of language. Both skills must be mastered by the EAL learner. The more adept they become at listening to spoken English and speaking it themselves, the easier it will be for you and they to cement your professional relationship. This will include the academic part – where you are teaching them a subject – and the non-academic part – where you are teaching rules and morals as well as communicating with them in a non-didactic sense.

It is likely that EAL learners will develop their spoken English in advance of their written English and that they will be able to listen to English with acuity well before they can read it with ease. This can cause a discrepancy about which you should be mindful. It is not one exclusive to EAL learners.

An individual – be they a student or an adult, someone for whom English is a first language or someone for whom it is a second language – may well be able to convey their thoughts more clearly and accurately in speech than in writing.

Speech is practised for long periods, every day. It is attended by a range of supplementary means of communication: facial expressions, body language, gestures, intonation, and volume. It can be modified in response to the audience. One phrase which is ubiquitous reads: 'Do you know what I mean?' Despite its overuse, it can nonetheless elicit important information. If the response is 'no' then we can try saying our piece again. We may even choose to say the same thing differently, or to give an example, or to make an analogy. This is not possible when writing.

The writer can edit their work, but any feedback they receive will be limited and after the event. This leads us on to an important point by which we must distinguish writing from speech.

Writing

Writing is a technology. It extends the reach of human beings in time and in space. It has much in common with speech, but it also has much that differs. We have already considered the example of instant modification. Let us look at some more:

- ◆ Writing requires something beyond the human body. This could be a pen, a piece of chalk, a computer, or whatever.
- ◆ Speech is ephemeral, writing is not. You or I could go and read the Dead Sea Scrolls, a collection of texts believed to be around

two thousand years old. We can never know anything of the conversations those who wrote them might have had.

♦ Writing is linear, whereas speech need not necessarily be so. Take a look at this book. See how the writing begins at the top left hand corner of the page, works its way across, and finally finishes at the bottom right hand corner of the page. Now imagine a conversation with a friend. You might 'go round in circles'. You might 'come straight to the point'. You might 'lose your point'. All these terms are metaphorical. Speech does not conform to geometry in the way writing must.

♦ Writing possesses fewer supplementary methods for specifying meaning. We have indicated how speech comes wrapped up in gesture, intonation, and so forth. Writing has punctuation. This is a much more limited system. Take the following sentence as an example: 'How did you find it?' On reading such a sentence, one is relying on the context being sufficiently accurate to convey the precise meaning (or for some additional text which explains, such as: 'she said menacingly'). Yet, if we heard such a phrase we would almost instantly recognise the meaning, most likely as a result of noticing where the speaker placed the stress.

♦ This leads us into reading. The contextual world in which a reader operates is vastly different to that which they work in when listening to speech. And it cannot be made up for by asking questions of clarification or requesting further information.

♦ In order to write accurately, in a way that conveys the meaning intended, one needs to understand certain conventions and be able to recall (or look up) words and phrases. In speech, the same does not apply. While a high value is placed on precise speech and certain settings require one to follow formal conventions, writing makes much heavier demands on the individual to conform and to be consistent with accepted usage. Again, the option to adjust, edit, rephrase, and recalibrate in the face of information received from the audience is simply not available.

The technological nature of writing should not be overlooked. Disentangling writing and speech, and making this explicit to students, is important. Many learners – EAL and others – quickly become demotivated when they find themselves without the deftness of touch which they have when speaking. The transfer of thought into visual language is taxing (remember, writing is visual), even more so if it is to be done accurately and precisely.

Reading

We come last to reading. Just as speaking and listening are joined, so are reading and writing. In each case we have a complementary pairing which covers the conveying of one's own thoughts and the reception of other people's.

Reading extends the cognitive capacity of humans well beyond that which writing on its own achieves. Possessing books equates to possessing a permanently accessible store of knowledge and ideas which exist independently of one's own mind. Libraries are the apotheosis of this fact; public or university collections offer thousands upon thousands of volumes, each one containing the thoughts of others made available through their having been written down.

A single example will suffice, one with which we are all familiar: the dictionary. Consider the absolute impossibility of an individual retaining the entirety of even a small version in their own mind. They may be able to use and explain most of the words such an edition would contain, but it is highly unlikely their recall would be comprehensive. What is more, they would almost certainly not be able to produce explanations as precise and specific for every word. Nor would they be able to ensure the consistency of these over time.

The dictionary provides each of us with an extension of our mental capacities. It allows us to check our understanding of words. It provides us with the meanings of new words we encounter. It gives examples of usage. It may point to synonyms or antonyms. Some versions will explain the origins of words and how their usage has altered over time.

The ability to read is like a key to an enormous stock of human knowledge. It allows us into the minds of others. In the case of fiction, we experience the imagination of people who we may never meet. Indeed, we can readily experience the imaginative landscapes of those who have been dead for centuries and more. The writings of Plato come from a civilisation eternally lost to us; the past is a place we cannot truly know. We can know *of* it, though, through reading those traces which remain.

Reading benefits from the logical structure of writing and its technical form. When reading we can revisit information at will, sure in the knowledge that it will remain identical to how it was when we first encountered it. This is not the case with speech, hence why it is always better to have a written contract than a verbal one.

We are also able to stop and return. Folding over the corner of a page or inserting a bookmark ensures we keep our place. We do not lose the moment as we might when speaking to someone. Nor do we run the risk of forgetting what was being conveyed; the information has already been written down and stored. The memory work is done for us by the fixing of the words in physical form.

When reading we have a greater expectation of sense and logic than when we are listening to someone. In the latter we do make these expectations, but they are caveated by the possibility of asking the speaker for clarification and relying upon the supplementary means of communication to disclose meaning. In addition, we will probably be more ready to fill in gaps in our understanding through (whether consciously or not) the use of assumptions or reference to prior experience.

Faced with a piece of text which is unclear, garbled, or seemingly nonsensical, we find ourselves without further immediate means by which to decode the writing. The means which *are* available – asking another person to read it and offer their opinion; writing to the author; researching, if possible, using other texts – are time-consuming, potentially indefinite (where *do* I look for the answer?), and do not presuppose the same likelihood of success as the methods employed to decode speech.

This is not to say that when we come to read a text we arrive as if from nowhere, without any prior knowledge or understanding. This is manifestly not the case. A reader seeks to contextualise the text in front of them by placing it within the mental maps they already have, by making connections to that which they already know, and by hypothesising interpretations which can be tested through further analysis.

The more one has read, the more one has thought about the written word and its relationship to reality, the more there is available to aid the development of understanding when encountering a new piece of writing. I say 'development of understanding' because it will often be the case that a reader will actively create meaning from a text rather than unlocking some definite meaning which has been put there by the author. It will depend, in part, on the genre, the author's purpose, and so forth. Yet, your reading of a text is unlikely to be identical to the next person's reading. It is all a matter of interpretation.

EAL learners are at a disadvantage when it comes to reading. In learning the language they are coming into contact with it for the first time. Therefore, they will be far behind their peers in terms of what they have read. Once they master the art of reading in English, they may well still lack some (or much) of the contextual apparatus which other students take for granted.

This difference will diminish as the learners develop their English skills (and context comes from experience as well as reading). Nonetheless, it is an important point to consider when asking EAL learners to work with written texts. On a side note, if we return to a continuum model, we might choose to view all of our learners as possessing relative levels of contextual understanding. The ability to access written information successfully is thus something we should be mindful about for our whole class.

Clarity, Accuracy, and Precision

Specific strategies, activities, and techniques for working with EAL learners follow this introduction. We may think briefly about general principles first. These inform the practical measures which come later.

Based on what has been said and what I presume you already know about EAL students, it is evident that clarity, accuracy and precision are of great importance when you are communicating in the classroom.

Clarity of language aids understanding. If you do not say or write what it is you mean to say, as simply as possible, you are giving your students more work to do. Simplicity does not mean as few words as possible – such an approach can be terse and unfriendly. What it does mean is using the amount of words necessary, no more and no less. This is not a figure which can be arrived at mathematically. It is a judgement on your part. Ask yourself whether what you are saying to students is sufficiently clear. If it is not, you may need to alter what you are saying or how you are saying it.

Minimising ambiguity is central to good teaching. This includes teaching EAL students. The teacher is on the wrong side of the numbers game in the classroom. They are on their own with perhaps twenty to thirty pupils in front of them. Each one needs to know what they are supposed to be doing. Each one is looking and listening separately. You, meanwhile, are alone, single and unitary. The worst possible situation is to have twenty to thirty voices crying out in discord: 'What do I do?' 'I don't understand what we are supposed to be doing.' 'Is this what you meant?'

To avoid such situations and to aid your EAL learners, think carefully before you speak, and spend time paring down the language on your resources. When giving instructions, do not begin until you know what you are going to say. It sounds obvious, yet it is a rule easily ignored. Many people will have a notion of what they wish to say but then find themselves lost, indulging in repetition, or saying something different to that which they intended. This can be avoided by taking a couple of seconds to flesh out in your head the specifics of what you want to communicate. You may even rehearse sentences prior to speaking them.

There will be times when it feels like you and your students are on different wavelengths. Remember, however, that the only control you have is over yourself. Get things right here and the rest will follow. Focussing on clarity will make you a better teacher in general, as well as with EAL learners specifically.

Accuracy and precision are two of the key elements which go to make up clarity. Think of accuracy as correctness and precision as exactness. The former requires you to ensure similarity between what you are thinking and what your language conveys to students. If you fail to specify the format in which you want something done and then complain when you receive posters instead of essays, the fault can be traced back to a lack of accuracy on your part. If you tell students to answer a question in whatever format they feel most comfortable with and this accords with your intentions, you are being accurate.

Accuracy helps create a better relationship between teacher and students because it minimises misunderstandings and helps pupils to understand the expectations you have of them. Such an atmosphere also gives you more time to work with students you have identified as needing your support, including EAL learners. By being accurate you are more in control of how you use your time during a lesson. You can therefore be more efficient.

Precision concerns your choice of words and the way in which you articulate them. You could accurately convey your meaning but do so in a long and unwieldy speech. Being precise means communicating your thoughts exactly as you intend them – and this means *as you intend them to be understood*. Excess language is the bane of good communication. It leads the listener astray and diminishes the impact of what you have said. You may still be able to communicate your meaning, but it will be less powerful and less persuasive because of your lack of precision.

Being precise means editing your speech and selecting the words which hold the exact meaning you intend them to hold. It means not repeating yourself unless it seems necessary and you consciously decide to do so. It may well be that with certain groups of students you will need to repeat yourself. This should be at your behest. Unconscious repetition is a sign that you are not really clear on what you are trying to say and have not considered what language will give the precise meaning you intend.

Being precise is vital if one wishes to minimise ambiguity. This is important for all learners, but especially for EAL students. They do not have the same means for filling in gaps or making assumptions about what you might be asking them to do. Look at the word 'might' in that last sentence. If your language leaves possibilities open that you have not intended, then you are making life harder for your students. An EAL learner is developing their understanding of English. The more precise and accurate is the language they see and hear in the classroom, the easier you are making it for them.

Clarity, precision, and accuracy: three words which should stay with you while you are teaching and creating resources. All your students will benefit, particularly those who are EAL learners. You may well find that it helps to minimise behaviour issues and increases motivation as well. There is a lot to be said for knowing where one stands and precisely what one is being asked for. It also makes it much easier to pull pupils up if they are not doing what they should be doing.

One final note on clarity and EAL learners, reinforcing the logic underpinning what has been stated. Our premises are as follows:

1. EAL learners are more likely to be positioned toward the 'newly encountering English' end of our continuum.
2. Their knowledge and understanding of English is likely to be at an earlier stage of development than that of their peers.
3. Their abilities in English in the four elements of language – speaking, writing, reading, and listening – will reflect point (2).

Therefore, to assist them, it is only right that we:

+ Make sure our language is clear and that it coveys exactly what we mean it to convey.
+ Model accurate and precise use of language so pupils are learning what is correct.
+ Minimise ambiguity so as to lower students' workload. This will allow them to concentrate on developing their understanding of what is said and written (rather than guessing at what is not said and not written). It will also help them to achieve success because the task of decoding is simpler. Success invariably aids motivation.

Conclusion

We have thought carefully about EAL learners and some aspects of our relationships with them. We have also thought about the nature of language and how it relates to and affects the individual who uses it. In so doing we have developed a nuanced picture of EAL learners and of language.

In addition, by suggesting a continuum perspective, indicating the similarities between EAL and non-EAL learners, and noting how the elements of language have facets and uses which are universal, we have intimated toward a style of teaching which sees all students as being in the process of language development. The needs students have are distinguished by the stage of development they find themselves at.

This approach is, I think, equitable, practical, and philosophically sound. It does not deny that EAL learners may require distinct support and that they lack at present some (or many) of the skills, knowledge, and understanding their peers take for granted. However, nor does it cleave them off into some separate group who may be marginalised because of the communication difficulties they are working to overcome.

It aims to treat EAL learners as individuals while still seeing them as part of the whole class. In turn, it sees the whole class as being in the process of language development, thus neutralising any notion that they have somehow 'done it' and require no further input from the teacher at the level of reading, writing, speaking, and listening.

Thinking in such a way negates many of the concerns we may have about meeting the needs of EAL learners when teaching whole-class or mixed-ability groups. This is because the underlying premise is that we are thinking about language anyway – ensuring it is an integral part of our teaching – and therefore helping EAL learners will involve doing what we do already, with some adaptations to recognise where they are on the continuum (and there are plenty enough of these contained within this book).

Further, taking such an approach in your classroom will convey to all of your students the normality of thinking about language, as well as the myriad ways in which we can develop our understanding of it. This is a good end in itself. In addition though, it should also help to stress the equality of all learners – regardless of where their English language skills are currently at.

Unfortunately, there is the potential for children (and adults) to fasten on difference and to see it in a negative light. Ensuring this does not happen, and that everyone in the classroom feels safe and secure, is important. Communicating a message of equality through your method sets the moral tone. Students will want to follow. If they do not, you have clearly set your stall out in advance and can admonish them accordingly.

To sum up, here is a checklist to bear in mind when working with EAL learners:

- EAL learners are, in many ways, just the same as the rest of your students.
- All learners respond to genuine praise.
- Making it clear why praise has been given aids learning.
- Genuine sympathy can help build rapport.
- Expect that you and your EAL learners will feel frustrated at times. Deal with this.
- All students are individuals.
- All students are at a different stage of language development.

- EAL learners are, generally, at an earlier stage of language development. They will therefore need extra, or different, support.
- Language consists of reading, writing, speaking, and listening.
- These four elements have similarities.
- They also differ in significant ways.
- Writing is a technology which has given rise to reading.
- Clarity, precision, and accuracy should be your watchwords in the classroom.
- Minimising ambiguity helps everybody.
- At all times your written and spoken language is a model for students.

And with all that in mind, on we go to the strategies, techniques, and activities.

CHAPTER TWO

Speaking and Listening

'No man is an island,' John Donne wrote. Language makes sure of it. Speaking affords the opportunity to articulate one's own thoughts such that others might be able to access them. Listening provides the opportunity to know the contents of minds other than one's own.

For most of us, the two skills are deeply ingrained; a fundamental aspect of who we are and how we experience the world. We use them over and over, day after day, with perhaps as little thought as we might give to the movements we make with our hands or the paces we take with our feet.

This can lead us to view speaking and listening as so much a part of us that further analysis would either be impossible (due to the lack of distance between ourselves and the object) or futile (because the two capacities are indivisible from our whole experience). But taking such a view is lazy and one we must be careful to warn against.

It is a tempting position to uphold, for sure. It negates any responsibility we might have for investigating speaking and listening in the classroom or for thinking about the efficacy of the speaking and listening we facilitate. Implicit in the view are the notions that these elements of language are in some way innate or that they are learnt independently of schooling (or that their development results from a mixture of both of these). In addition, there is the idea that skill and dexterity in these areas advance in the course of life as it is lived, not in the classroom. Set against this is the learning of writing and reading which needs to be contrived because of its separateness, its technological extension of men's and women's capabilities. We are born possessing vocal cords, but without a pen.

There is some truth in these arguments. As we noted in the introduction, the complementary pairings – speaking and listening, reading and writing – do differ significantly. This includes the fact that the former is a function of the body and the mind alone (but with other individuals inherent to its development) and that the latter is an extension of this process with the addition of physical objects beyond the mind and body (writing implements and written media).

It is clear as well that speaking and listening do develop in 'the natural course of things'. Parents speak to their children from the moment they are born. They continue to do this throughout their child's upbringing (it is hoped). As the child ages, so they are able to begin mimicking the sounds they hear. Time progresses, and they come to associate meaning with the sounds. Eventually they are able to manipulate these sounds sufficiently well to speak and listen with ease. Clearly this process, universal and profound, precedes any experience of education and always has done.

Nonetheless, even with all these propositions accepted and agreed upon, the conclusion ought not to be that speaking and listening can be glossed over in the classroom. We should consider some of the reasons behind this before we go on to strategies, techniques, and activities intended to assist EAL learners.

Why Think Critically About Speaking and Listening in the Classroom?

Speech can provide an important, and at times necessary, prelude to writing. Two people in discussion over some topic are both trying to make clear what it is they think so that the other can understand them. In such situations, mediation takes place. That which one knows inside one's head needs to be made known outside of there. The speaker thus has to think about what words will express their thoughts most clearly. They will then use the information provided by their partner (facial expressions, gestures, questions, and so on) to adapt this choice of words, if need be.

Because speech comes to us before writing, and because, for young people particularly, it is likely to be the easier of the two mediums for us to use, speaking our thoughts prior to writing them can be a great boon. It displaces some of the mental effort required to make our internal experiences communicable. Speaking about an idea before writing about it means you are arriving at the writing having already started articulating your thoughts. The additional demands which writing makes (compared to speech) are therefore following fewer demands than if there had been no prior speaking.

Of course, there are also times when we do not consciously know what we think about a subject. Or, it may be that we are unable to provide an answer to a problem because none immediately presents itself. To go straight into writing in such a situation may be doubly difficult. In such setting, the space, freedom, and flexibility speaking provides helps individuals to develop their thoughts. Here, speaking about a topic constructs one's understanding of that topic. This might include an identification of the areas in which one is ignorant or uncertain. In any case, this is much harder for most students to do through writing.

Whenever we speak, we overcome the isolation of human existence. This may sound a little over the top. After all, do we not live in societies and come from families? Is not human existence predicated on kinship and dependence? Well yes, but this does not disguise the fact that each of us is separate and that who one is, is who one is and no more. Certainly, we may conceive of ourselves as being intimately bound up with others, perhaps even to the extent that our very self feels as if it is made up not *just of ourselves* but of others as well. We would feel sympathy for the person who has nobody but themselves. Most of us know the psychological pain which comes from the death of a loved one: 'It is like losing a part of oneself' so the saying goes, and so would many attest, myself included.

Nonetheless, it remains true to say that a human being is physically constituted within the body they inhabit. It is communication which allows us to transcend this. For most, this comes in the form of speaking and listening (though this is not the only way). In any classroom there are times for silence; independent work necessitates stillness and concentration. However, just as important is the development of rapport between students and the establishing of working relationships. Speaking and listening are an integral part of this.

Giving students structured space in which to communicate with one another helps to develop a positive atmosphere. It can create a sense of belonging and commonality between members of the group, as well as diminishing uncertainty (which may breed other, more negative attitudes).

How you plan, direct, and regulate the speaking and listening will be crucial. Students may take opportunities to talk about things other than the work. You will have to judge how much of this you are prepared to let go (if any). The criteria could be to what extent off-topic chat is beneficial to rapport and relationship building and whether this outweighs the time spent not on task.

Listening to someone speak is akin to being taken into a small but important area of their mind. Small because speech is the end point of that teeming mass of ideas and experience we all possess. Important because it is the part we choose to share with others.

Having a conduit to other people's minds helps us to retain levity when dealing with our own feelings and when developing our own thoughts. It allows us to know the feelings and thoughts of others. This is an important end in itself as well as being the gateway to sympathy, empathy, and compassion. There is also the fact that what others say may challenge what we claim to know or believe. At best, this will cause us to defend our notions or to look at them more critically. Both these avenues may be left untrodden if we merely keep to ourselves.

Listening provides us with information. In the classroom this could take many forms. For example:

- Knowledge about the world (usually delivered as knowledge about a certain topic or subject)
- Knowledge about rules and morals
- The opinions different people hold
- What others think about any of the above

The list goes on. Suffice to say, what students do with the information they gather ought to be a matter of interest to us as teachers.

Listening, in its broadest sense, can be divided into two categories: active and passive. In the latter, what we hear washes over us. We are inert, a rock upon which waves are breaking. We might be able to take in a lot of information this way and later recall the things which were said. Unless we actually think about this information and interact with it mentally, however, what we are learning is the knowledge someone else possesses. We are not making our own understanding. Instead, we are borrowing and assimilating someone else's.

Of itself this is not a problem. Especially if we are confident in the authority and expertise of the speaker concerning the matter on which they are speaking. Yet, I would propose that there is a qualitative difference between this form of learning and that which comes through active listening. It is the difference between knowing and understanding.

We might be able to give an account of how something works, based on a recollection of what we have been told. This would not mean, though, that we understand how it is that it works. It would mean that we know what we have been told about how it works. In order to say we understand how it works we would have to engage actively with what we have heard (or go and find out for ourselves by investigating whatever the thing in question is). This active engagement may be as simple as attending to the words of the speaker and using logic, reason, or experience to test their validity. On a deeper level, it might mean analysing what has been said and seeing if it accords with other information we already know, or whether we can connect it to existing pieces of understanding we possess. A third example of active listening would be the use of analogy to 'place' the information we are hearing within a framework with which we are already familiar.

The extent to which any of these processes leads us to *truly* understand what is being said is debatable. What is clear, though, is that active listening involves the listener's mind doing things to that which they hear. This doing leads to understanding above and beyond the basic recall which is a consequence of passive listening.

It should also be clear that active and passive listening are not two separate and distinct processes; as with our model of language development, the best way to conceive of them is as opposite ends of a continuum.

All this should give us cause to consider the efficacy, in terms of learning, of the speaking and listening which goes on in our classrooms. The more we can encourage students to listen actively, the more likely they are to develop their understanding.

The teacher's role in facilitating speaking and listening encompasses a great deal. You will need to think about how much you are prepared to intervene in discussion; whether talk is to be highly structured or placed inside a loose framework; what type of activities will you use – paired, group, or whole-class discussions, for example. You will also need to consider what the purpose of speaking and listening is in your lessons and whether or not you will communicate this to your students. There might be times when to do so would impair the naturalness of their conversation. On other occasions it may be vital to make it clear why something is happening and how students should act to ensure its success.

There is more we could say about speaking and listening, but we have said enough to indicate why it is an area of classroom practice worthy of critical consideration. In so doing, it has been implicit that this extends to teaching EAL learners. Everything noted above is of relevance to them, just as it is relevant to any other student. That their abilities in the English language may be behind those of their peers makes it all the more pressing that we as teachers attend to their experience of speaking and listening. The activities, strategies, and techniques which follow will help you to do just that.

Speaking and Listening Activities, Strategies, and Techniques

1. Buddy-Up
Explanation and Rationale

In any class there will be students at different stages of language development. Some will be relatively advanced for their age, perhaps surpassing most of their peers in terms of eloquence and articulacy. These students can help the whole group to develop. Their use of language can provide a model for other pupils, supplementing that which you are providing. This may involve them being asked to share their written work or, if they are strong orally, being encouraged to contribute to or lead whole-class and group discussions. There will be reciprocal benefits, as the student is given opportunities to showcase and hone their skills in front of an audience.

It can be a good idea to pair EAL learners with pupils who have strong speaking and listening skills. This buddying-up can be direct or indirect. If direct, you might ask your non-EAL student to help your EAL learner through modelling good speaking and listening. You might also ask them to talk more with the EAL learner than they normally would with other students, so as to give them further practice in speaking and listening in English. It might be helpful to explain to your EAL pupil that the person you are asking them to work with has shown great skill in using the English language. This, you can add, will be helpful in guiding them and assisting them in their development.

Alternatively, you may prefer to leave the buddying-up implicit and indirect. This will involve you pairing an EAL learner with a strong speaker and listener but not giving a particular rationale for the decision to the students. If anything is said, you can point to the fact that all students are asked to work in pairs for particular tasks. Depending on the characters and personalities involved, you may deem it better to use this deception than to explain why you have asked certain students to work together.

Example One

Sit EAL learners beside students who model good speaking and listening. Build a series of discussion tasks into your lessons in which students talk in pairs or small groups. Each time such an activity comes up, your EAL learners will have the benefit of their partner's expertise.

Example Two

Sit EAL learners beside students who model good speaking and listening. Explain to the students that you would like them to talk through their ideas before they start any tasks. Point out that this will help them to get their own thoughts clear as well as to consider the thoughts of others. In addition, the EAL learner will be in a position to repeatedly practise speaking and listening about whatever topic is under consideration.

Example Three

Choose a student who has strong speaking and listening skills and ask them to buddy-up with an EAL learner who is new to the class. Explain that you would like them to help the learner settle in and that they should try to support them in getting used to the class and the lessons. This 'induction' process will be beneficial to the EAL learner. It will also give them an opportunity to experience strong speaking and listening and act as a reward of responsibility for the other student.

2. Role Models

Explanation and Rationale

Group work can be a double-edged sword. On the one hand, it provides students with opportunities to speak and listen to one another, to think actively about the topic you are studying, and to work independently of the teacher. On the other hand, it has the potential to degenerate into social discussion, can be difficult to regulate, and can lack structure, something which can be problematic for many students.

With good planning you can avoid these potential drawbacks. What is more, consistent use of well-planned group work should help your students to become more familiar with what is involved and thus better placed to get the most out of it.

If you have EAL learners in your class, you should include them in your group work planning. Specifically, this ought to involve you making sure they have the opportunity to interact with students who will be good role models for speaking and listening. By doing this, you will be helping your learners to make progress in their English development. In addition, they should be in a position to pick up some of the 'hidden' rules of language which students use both inside and outside of the classroom.

Example One

If you have more than one EAL learner in your class, it may be helpful to place them in different groups. This way, you will be maximising their exposure to accomplished English speakers and, if the groups are constructed carefully, strong role models. You might make adjustments based on the relative capacities of the EAL learners. For example, if one is at a higher stage of development than the other, it might be less pressing for them to be with a number of strong role models. Perhaps one will be sufficient, freeing up more for the student whose skills are weaker at present.

Example Two

This method of grouping allows EAL learners to experience a range of strong role models in one discussion activity. Split the class into groups, ensuring you distribute your strongest speakers and listeners evenly. Give each group a question to discuss. After sufficient time has elapsed, choose one member from each group to stand up (here you will choose some, or perhaps all, of your strongest speakers and listeners). Ask the people who have stood up to find a new group and to take their question with them. The reconstituted groups then discuss the new questions. Repeat the process as many times as you wish.

Example Three

If EAL learners are at an early stage of development, it may be that their speaking and listening is in advance of their reading and writing.

Rather than working against this, work with it. During certain written tasks, you might group EAL learners with strong speaking and listening role models and ask them to discuss the topic instead. You could ask the group to work towards a joint written response, while still making clear the emphasis for them is on talking.

3. Rehearsal

Explanation and Rationale

Stage fright is a common enough anxiety among the general population. Many people dread the thought of having to speak in front of a crowd, let alone having to recite passages from memory. For some, the apprehension which comes with being asked to present to others – be it at school, at work, or elsewhere – can be immobilising. For others, the task is not easy but they soldier on regardless and are relieved to reach the end, upon which they hasten from the limelight as quickly as possible.

Rehearsing is one of the best ways to overcome the anxiety which can accompany speaking in public. By practising what one intends to say, the act of saying it becomes easier. There are a few reasons for this. First, rehearsing gives one the opportunity to go over one's thoughts and to experience the speaking of them. This means the public act is a repetition, rather than a first time. Second, and linked to this, is the point that having attended to the nature and content of what one intends to say, the brain does not have to attend to the ordering of thoughts upon the saying of them. The hard work has been done already, giving more space to think about the other things which are going on. Finally, familiarity breeds confidence. Rehearsal before the event means the event is not unique. It is no longer a one-time occasion which will succeed or fail. Instead, it becomes just another opportunity to articulate what one has already been over. One feels more confident as a result.

All of this is apt for EAL learners speaking English in lessons. Here are some examples of how to apply the observations.

Example One

Let EAL learners know in advance when you will come to them for answers. For example, you might talk to them about the plenary before introducing it to the rest of the class and give them extra time in which to think about and practise their response. This method helps EAL learners to take part in activities and speak publicly in the classroom. It

acknowledges that they may need additional time to formulate and prepare their answers.

Example Two

When setting your whole class a question, such as during a discussion, give everybody time in which to rehearse their answers. This might
see you posing the question and then asking everyone to discuss their
thoughts in pairs before practising a final, succinct answer ready to share
with the whole class. Here, everyone is given the opportunity to rehearse,
including your EAL learners.

Example Three

When students are engaged in a task, work individually with your EAL
learners. Speak with them about the topic under consideration and ask
them questions which you will later ask the whole class. Once students
have talked their answers through with you, ask them if they are prepared
to share them in the whole-class discussion which is to follow. Even if
they are not, you could recount their ideas, praising them in the process.
This should help develop the students' confidence.

4. Model Speaking and Listening

Explanation and Rationale

Watching two participants engaged in a high-class debate can be cap-
tivating. If you find yourself in the position of seeing such a thing live,
rather than on the television, it can feel as if there is electricity in the air,
generated by the verbal sparring of the speakers. Should both of them
get fully drawn into the argument, the drama of the analytical back-and-
forth can grow and grow, enthralling the audience as the narrative of the
discussion unfolds before them.

If you attend carefully to such a display, it is possible to pick out rhetor-
ical techniques which can be fairly easily mimicked, ways of constructing
verbal arguments, and means of dealing with counterarguments. This
fact – being able to assimilate elements of the speaking and listening we
observe – is also true for the classroom.

We have indicated the benefits of buddying-up EAL learners with
strong speakers and listeners. The teacher also has an important role to
play in modelling speaking and listening. After all, it is the teacher who
knows exactly what they want their students to achieve. And it is the

teacher who is in a position to make this happen and to demonstrate what it might look like.

Example One

When setting up a task which involves speaking and listening, model precisely what it is you want your students to do. An example of this would be to take a student whom you know is capable and confident enough to hold a conversation with you and proceed to act out the task with them for the benefit of the rest of the class. While you do this, you could refer to certain aspects of what you are doing. For example, you might draw attention to the way in which you are listening or to how you are taking account of what you hear when you give your own responses.

Example Two

Sit your class in a circle. Place two chairs facing each other in the middle of the circle. Sit in one of the chairs and ask a strong speaker and listener to occupy the one opposite. Model a discussion, based on the topic you are studying. Stop at intervals and ask students in the circle to explain what is being done well, and why it is good. You could have a scribe who notes down all the points raised. Students then have their own discussions in which they try to apply some of the good practice which has been identified.

Example Three

Once the activity has been set up and the class is engaged in paired or group discussion, go and work directly with EAL learners and their partners or groups. Choose certain aspects of speaking and listening – for example, questioning, responding to points, or using technical vocabulary – and ask the students to focus on replicating that skill successfully. Tell them to show you when they have achieved this. If you are satisfied, repeat the process, but this time focus on a different aspect of speaking and listening. You could continue to do this, flitting between groups or pairs which include an EAL learner. It is a good way to provide targeted, personalised support.

5. Speaking and Listening Success Criteria

Explanation and Rationale

It can be hard to achieve success, although it is much harder if you do not know what the criteria are against which you are being judged. An athlete, for example, trains with a clear end in mind: they know what the requirements of their event or sport are, and they know what standard they will have to meet in order to be deemed successful. This standard may be a rough one (as in Sunday league football) or a precise one (as in the final of the Olympic 1500 metres).

If an athlete were told to train, but the nature of what they were training for was not revealed to them, they would be in a quandary. Do they take a risk and try to guess what particular demands will be made of them, or do they aim for the middle and seek to ensure a high level of general fitness? The latter option is certainly the safer and may well result in reasonable results. Even without knowing the specific end, an athlete would be aware that they needed to be physically fit, flexible, mentally tough, and so on.

In the classroom, with students replacing athletes, success in speaking and listening has the potential to be equally uncertain. Using success criteria is a means of getting away from this. By sharing with pupils what it is they are being judged against, everyone gets a clear sense of what the expectations are and how it is they can be met. What is more, success criteria will reveal the different elements of speaking and listening which are seen as important.

Example One

EAL learners may not be able to access the same success criteria as other learners in the class. It will depend on the stage of language development they are at. Therefore, it might be useful to provide them with a separate set of criteria, based on an assessment of their current capabilities. Alternatively, you could give them a wide set of criteria which you would like them to meet over an extended period (a term, for example). You and the student could review progress at certain points, with the learner keeping hold of the criteria for reference purposes.

Example Two

Use pictures to supplement any written success criteria you provide. This will help EAL learners to grasp the meaning of what you have written or said. Simple examples include a question mark to signify asking questions and an ear with a hand cupped to it to signify sustained listening.

Example Three

Identify students who have met the success criteria. Ask them to repeat their performances for the whole class. You and they can then explain why what they did was good. A development of this is to ask those students who meet the criteria to work with EAL learners, showing them what they have done. It is important that the link between their actions and the success criteria is made explicit. This will help students who are learning English to equate what they have seen with the written or spoken criteria which have been indicated.

6. Listening Frames
Explanation and Rationale

When dealing with any piece of text, one is forever safe in the knowledge that, at any point, reference could be made to what has already been read. Take a detective novel, for example. If one were to forget the background of a character currently under suspicion, and this information had been provided at an earlier point, the simple remedy would be to revisit the appropriate section in the book. Equally, if one were reading an academic article and became lost in the author's subclauses, the natural reaction would be to return to the beginning of the paragraph or section and begin again.

The written word is fixed. It is contained within a physical medium and is itself a physical object. If you display your instructions for students on your whiteboard, those students will be able to look at them again and again without any alteration taking place. What is more, they will know that such a situation will continue to prevail. Such is the nature of the written word.

Speech does not share these facets. As a result, it can be harder to analyse, particularly for students who are at an early stage of language development. Due to their lack of familiarity with English they may be at a disadvantage when trying to analyse the spoken word because their focus is still on decoding meaning in a basic sense. This, logically, must come before any other type of analysis. After all, if we do not know what words mean, then how can we start to analyse them?

Listening frames offer support to students in such situations. They can help to make connections between written words and speech, aid the process of decoding, or take away some of the analytical burden.

Example One

Provide EAL learners with a worksheet on which you have printed a range of key words relevant to the lesson. Ask the students to place a tick or tally mark every time they hear one of the words (this relies on students already knowing how to say the words). A listening frame along these lines will help students to familiarise themselves with the relationship between how words are written and how they are spoken. It will also give the students a specific focus for their listening. This will help to direct their time in the classroom and give them a sense of purpose. You could ask a fluent English speaker to help a learner who is using such a frame, or you yourself could keep visiting them to speak about their progress.

Example Two

Provide EAL learners with a worksheet containing a range of words which you will use in the lesson or which you anticipate will be used in student discussions. Give a definition for each of these words, an appropriate image, or both. Ask pupils to listen out for the words and make a tally or tick when they hear them. Each time they do this, they should also reacquaint themselves with the meaning of the word. In essence, this listening frame is a little like a glossary designed for the specific lesson you are teaching.

Example Three

Provide EAL learners with a worksheet in which the areas to be discussed are clearly delineated. For example, in a lesson on rivers you may put the subheadings: Types of Rivers; Places Where We Find Rivers; Uses of Rivers. This creates a note-taking frame for the students. It breaks down the discussion (or teacher exposition) which is to come, meaning the students do not have to. It is removing some of the analytical burden by providing a ready-made structure. You may further help students by signalling (or asking other students to signal) when the talk is moving from one area to the next.

7. Purposeful Talk

Explanation and Rationale

We have noted the power of talk to help individuals formulate ideas, articulate thoughts, and refine their own thinking. In order for students to achieve these ends in the classroom it is important that the talk which takes place is purposeful. Discussion or debate which does not have a reason behind it lacks a sense of direction. With no clear end point in mind, it is difficult for students to judge whether they are doing what is expected of them or not. They may also question the validity of the activity because they cannot 'see' its point. This can lead to disengagement, lack of focus, and recourse to social conversations.

It may be that the teacher does not communicate to students why it is they are being asked to talk to one another. A worse situation is when the teacher does not know what the purpose of the discussion or debate is. They may then begin to question what exactly it is they have asked pupils to do. If the teacher cannot explain the reasoning behind the activity they have selected, then they will not be able to share this with students. Nor will they be able to assess whether the talk is working or not. They will simply have no reference point against which to make a judgement.

Considering the purpose of talk in the classroom is vital. Teachers should be able to explain what is to be gained from a talk-based activity, and, generally, it is better to share the reasoning with students. This applies to EAL learners particularly because the talk they are being asked to do may have quite specific purposes, perhaps different to other pupils. In addition, the effort EAL learners are putting into their speaking and listening will be strained by the extra requirement of having to try to determine why they are doing what they are doing in the first place.

Example One

When introducing any speaking and listening activity, make it clear what you want students to do and why. Demonstrate what the results should look like (or sound like) and why these should be deemed as good. Before starting the activity, check that what you have said has been understood. This includes checking with EAL learners. Leave some brief instructions on the board which students can refer to or which you can use if you notice any pupils going off task.

Example Two

Identify what you would like your EAL learners to get out of the speaking and listening they are doing in class. For example, you may want them to practice using key words or to identify arguments they hear other students making. Talk to your EAL learners individually and explain what you have decided upon. Indicate that they should see discussion activities as an opportunity to practise that particular thing.

This approach can be developed by putting together a checklist of different options and asking your EAL learners which they would like to focus on in a particular lesson. Over a series of lessons they can cycle through the options on the list.

Example Three

Set a target which you want learners to achieve through talking. An example would be the creation of a mind map which contains the thoughts of all the members of a group concerning a certain subject. Tell your class that they should signal when they have achieved this. You can then go and check whether you agree. This is helpful to EAL learners because it makes the purpose of the talk clearer and gives them a tangible endpoint. The approach can be developed by providing a range of targets that get progressively more difficult. By careful pairing and grouping, EAL learners should be able to scale the ladder with the support of their peers.

8. The Rules of Talk

Explanation and Rationale

We have looked at the uses of speaking and listening success criteria and thought about how these can benefit students, particularly those who are learning English as an additional language. The present strategy – The Rules of Talk – shares some similarities with that approach. It makes explicit recourse to the expectations which should guide any talk which goes on in the classroom. It differs sufficiently, however, to warrant a separate entry here.

Success criteria look at what the teacher and their students are aiming to achieve by using talk in the classroom. The Rules of Talk focusses on the often implicit expectations participants bring to conversations. The former is a guiding purpose based on the requirements of an individual lesson or activity. The latter are cultural norms which may be rarely articulated; they will often be learnt unwittingly, or through the wider process of socialisation, during an individual's development.

For an EAL learner, the rules governing different types of talk may be hard to grasp. The culture in which they grew up may possess different rules or different manners or modes of talking. For most native speakers, the rules will be second nature. Things which they take for granted may be confusing to EAL learners. For example, formal debates operate on an antagonistic premise. One side is in favour and one side is against. If a learner has not come across formal debates before, they cannot be expected to know the rules which govern this particular mode of speaking and listening. Similarly, discussion of sensitive topics may make extensive use of hypothetical examples and composite characters. An EAL learner who was not made aware of this may become confused as to the subject of discussion or as to what is seen as appropriate material to share with the group.

Example One

When you introduce a discussion activity for the first time, ask some of the fluent English speakers in your class to explain how the activity works. They could do this through a short summary or by modelling the particular activity. Ask them to make explicit the rules and norms which govern the talk. This could be done through a comparison to other types of talk or by an identification of the three things which distinguish that particular activity from other activities. Once this has been done, speak to your EAL learners and assess whether they have understood what has been explained.

Example Two

Decide on a small number of talk-based activities you will use (between three and five) over the course of a term or longer. Introduce these activities one at a time, giving students space in which to get familiar with each one. Identify the rules which govern talk in each type of activity. Make these clear to students. This could involve listing the rules and providing appropriate visual reminders. Operating in this way should ensure EAL learners are made aware of the norms relevant to different activities. They will also have time in which to assimilate the rules for each type of talk before being introduced to the next activity.

Example Three

Put EAL learners in groups or pairs that will see them working with sympathetic, supportive peers who have strong speaking and listening skills. Indicate to the fluent students that you would like them to help the EAL learners get a better understanding of what different talk-based activities require. Ask them to work through the activities with the EAL learners while, at the same time, explaining how the activities function and how one should go about speaking and listening when taking part in them. You may want to assist by sitting-in with a pair or group and supporting the explanations which are given.

9. Atmosphere

Explanation and Rationale

Getting the atmosphere right in the classroom is a fine art, not least when one is making good use of speaking and listening. Such an approach is likely to see more transitions between activities. Students will be working independently in pairs or groups, using talk to create knowledge, to refine knowledge, and to develop understanding. This requires the teacher to cede a good deal of control. Interactions move from pupil-teacher to pupil-pupil. While the teacher can circulate in order to assess and regulate learning, responsibility is given to students to lead themselves and meet the expectations which have been set out.

By attending to the atmosphere which prevails in your classroom, you can help to ensure that when students *are* working independently there is a greater chance of them being successful. Your speaking and listening goals are more likely to be met when the atmosphere is positive and students see respect of people's opinions, and their differences, as a given. Continually working to develop and reinforce such an atmosphere will result in it becoming a norm. Students will expect this to be the way things are – whoever is leading the learning.

If you persist in this, and remain consistent in promoting the atmosphere you want (which includes admonishing behaviour which is not in line with your expectations), then your students are more likely to internalise the behaviours which go towards engendering such an atmosphere. This is a step on from recognising what the norms of a classroom are, because it involves the students assimilating those norms and coming to see them as a part of themselves, not just a temporary way of acting which they consent to when necessary. This whole approach will benefit EAL learners as well as the rest of your students. Here are some methods you can use to help make it happen.

Example One

Setting up rules and expectations with a class is a strategy familiar to most teachers. A development of this is to set up specific speaking and listening rules. These can take account of the requirements of successful speaking and listening, as well as the different responsibilities which students will have when taking part in classroom talk. Agreeing on these with your class helps add weight to the authority which the rules possess. You can use them yourself in various ways. For example: asking students to model the rules for newcomers (like EAL learners who join midway through a year); refer groups who are not working as you would wish to the rules, and give specific praise highlighting individuals who are following the rules and why this is leading to positive outcomes for them.

Example Two

Discuss the purpose of speaking and listening as it relates to learning. Talking about the pedagogical reasoning informing the use of speaking and listening with students provides them with a rationale as to why they should take it seriously. Knowing the meaning behind something makes it comprehensible. This means it is more likely that students will accept the importance of a positive atmosphere when they are talking with one another. Admonishing inappropriate behaviour with sound reasoning, of which pupils are already aware, is also a powerful means of getting students back on track. Unlike appeals to good nature and so forth, it is exceptionally difficult to argue with.

Example Three

Use students as peer practitioners. This method sees the class policing its own behaviour and therefore working independently to regulate the atmosphere. Identify two or three students who can act as 'Speaking and Listening Champions (or some other superlative)'. They will monitor the behaviour of their peers and model excellent speaking and listening. You may want to rotate who it is that takes on these roles; this gives you the opportunity to encourage students to try to earn the right.

Ways in which Speaking and Listening Champions can be used include circulating and regulating behaviour according to rules and expectations, supporting EAL learners, checking up on how EAL learners are doing, acting as buddies for EAL learners, and being identified as speaking and listening specialists whom anyone (including EAL learners) can go to for support.

10. Listening Assistance
Explanation and Rationale

Listening can be a strenuous business. There is the matter of decoding meaning, of sustaining attention, and of assessing the value of what is being said. One must also try to gauge the speaker's intentions, identify whether what they are saying coheres with how they are saying it (including their body language), and ascertain whether it connects with what one already knows. In the case of a student for whom English is an additional language, juggling all these different tasks is likely to be difficult.

Given that a speaker has the express intention of getting their meaning across to those who are listening, it is reasonable to assume that they will be prepared to make certain adaptations which will assist the listeners. Sometimes these will be unconscious, for example when someone leans forward involuntarily in order to emphasise a point. On other occasions they will be contrived or even scripted, such as when a politician uses gestures in accordance with the findings of psychological studies. Either way, the speaker is taking steps to assist the listener.

Taking the latter approach – the conscious adapting of one's voice and body while speaking – can be helpful in the classroom. If whoever is speaking, be it the teacher or a student, thinks about how they might assist the listener, then the communication of meaning is likely to be made easier. Given that you are going to be working with students at early stages of language development, promoting an attitude of assistance in your classroom will be beneficial. There are many ways in which speakers might assist listeners; here are some examples which you yourself can use and which you can talk about with your students.

Example One

Look at students when you are talking to them and make sure they are looking at you. It sounds obvious. It is obvious! Yet, with all the potential distractions which can come our way while we are teaching, it is quite possible that we will continue talking to a student while turned away from them. It is much easier to listen to someone if they are looking at you. One can follow the movements of the speaker's lips, as well as analyse the expressions they make with their face. For EAL learners who are still getting to grips with English, having a speaker look directly at them can be a major help in their efforts to understand what is being said.

Example Two

Use your body to supplement your speech. For example, if you say a size, mirror that size with your hands; spread your palms wide apart to indicate 'big', or squeeze your thumb and forefinger close together to signify 'small'. Another example is to emphasise points by stepping forward or pointing one's hands in the direction of the audience (as if to say 'this is the important bit'). Try to work such gestures into your performance so that they appear natural. If you feel uncomfortable with them, you will probably appear stilted and lack the certainty which a strong gesture ought to possess. Nonetheless, by trying to bring supplemental gestures alongside your speech you will be attempting to assist the listener. Practice will lead to improvement.

Example Three

Ensure what you say is interesting, useful, and relevant (or, ideally, all three). This will assist the students who are listening to you in three ways. First, it will give them a reason to listen, and, as such, their motivation will increase because they will feel there is something in it for them. Second, it will require you to think about what you are saying in advance (as you have a set of criteria to try to meet). This means that what you say is likely to be clear and considered. Listeners will therefore have to expend less energy trying to decode what you are saying. Third, it will connect to things which the students already know. This will help them to contextualise your speech; they will be able to relate it to their existing understanding.

These three examples have been written with the teacher in mind. They apply to the speaking which students do as well. Analyse your own speech when speaking to pupils, and highlight different aspects of what you are doing. Students can then try to copy your example when they speak. This trickle-down approach has the potential to get all members of your class thinking about how they can assist listeners when they are speaking. The benefits for all students, including EAL learners, will soon follow.

CHAPTER THREE

Images

Some years ago I was first introduced to the paintings of JMW Turner. At that time I knew little about the background to his works or the historical context in which they had been created. Nor did I know much about the man himself, the history of art in general, or even the ways in which artists went about experimenting with different materials and modes of composition. I knew little about the 'ways of seeing' artists possess or how they seek to convey these through their works.

Yet none of this mattered as I stood looking at the paintings of light and landscape hung on the walls before me. It felt as if I were falling into the majesty of celestial scenes wrung out of the commonplace world in which men and women tread. It was as if the canvases were suffused with emotion, painted with twin brushes, one real and one ghostly. The colour spread across the surface while the feelings of the artist, channelled through the divine, were entwined with the paintings by threads of heaven, unseen yet strongly felt.

When I look at Turner's paintings today I still get the same sense of nature recast in the light – real and ethereal – of nascent spirituality. Whether this was intended by the artist and whether other people would see his work in the same way is immaterial. What is clear is the latent power to draw thought and emotion from the viewer which images possess.

Upon coming across a picture or drawing, one is looking at another person's mediation of experience. A photograph captures the world as it was once seen; in painting, an artist transfers from their mind what it is they see. Both make a view of things, an image based in the world or the mind, available to others.

The structure of the image plays a major role in the meaning which it conveys or which it might evoke. An abstract painting, for example, may be intended to speak more about the relationship between colour, form, and shape than a portrait, in which those elements are subjugated to the communication of the subject's appearance (or the artist's interpretation of their appearance). Even so, the viewer will not necessarily take the same meaning from the image as that which the artist set out to convey. Equally, the artist may aim to sustain multiple meanings within the same piece of work, happily leaving it up to the viewer to tease these out or project their own.

These thoughts connect to our topic of using images to help EAL learners in so much as they indicate that the interaction between viewer and image is not straightforward, yet is often powerful. This could manifest itself in a number of ways. For me, Turner makes plain in his paintings things which I feel about the world but which I do not have the words to say. Even with page after page of writing arranged with the greatest care and consideration, I doubt I would be able to come close to encapsulating what it is that, for me, is given voice through his work.

Visual media offers a different way of communicating to that provided by written and spoken language. It possesses a different structure and a different logic to the word; it can 'say' things far more quickly, or in much less space; it can articulate a feeling or a thought which is not amenable to language; it can move us closer to being able to enunciate an idea, prodding us in a certain direction or making connections for us which, at present, remain one step beyond our linguistic capacities.

It is wise to be aware of the power of images when working in the classroom. Day-to-day we are not going to seek a procession of experiences like the one I outlined above. Even if it were possible to create such experiences at will, the results would be overwhelming. There would be no time to process the information or to reflect on its causes or meaning.

What we can do, though, is use images as another means of communication. In so doing, we are acknowledging the premises which I have alluded to: (i) visual media can convey meaning and (ii) visual media conveys meaning differently from written and spoken language.

If the second were not true, there would be no point discussing visual media in the context of EAL learners. If the first were not true, there would be no point discussing visual media at all.

Perhaps the most useful role which pictures can play in the classroom, particularly when working with EAL students, is as supplements to written and spoken words. A supplement is something which is in addition to something else. Think of the Sunday supplements which come with the main section of the newspaper. The main section is available every day and forms the continuous output through the week. The supplements are produced in addition to this. They arrive at the weekend when people have more free time and are able to read at leisure.

Pictures can supplement the words you use when speaking to students or when giving them written information. You probably do this to some extent already when creating your resources. For example, if you use PowerPoint slides to structure your lessons, you may well include clip art or pictures from the internet to illustrate some of the things you mention.

The great advantage which images hold over language is that they do not require the same prior learning. A student who has just arrived in your classroom with no knowledge of English will nonetheless be able to understand pictures of things with which they are already familiar.

Images can guide learners. Even if they are not in a position to access the meaning of what is being said in the classroom, a relevant image can make it clear what topic is being discussed. This provides some purchase for the learner, who can call up what they know about the subject indicated. They can then think about this in their first language or through whatever standard of English they currently possess.

Using pictures as guides also helps EAL learners to feel included in what is going on. There is something which they can decode and think about regardless of their present stage of English. Finally, the use of images as guides helps EAL learners by prompting them to connect what they are hearing, and the written words they are seeing, with that particular area of thought and the world signified by the image. It directs the linguistic assimilation and interaction in which they are engaged, immersed as they are in the language of the classroom.

Images contextualise words. This can be broad or specific; one example of each will suffice. Studying the topic of Henry VIII, one might choose to contextualise the language broadly by displaying images of kings from a variety of different cultures, both real and fictional. There could also be pictures of leaders, expanding the theme beyond that of monarchy. On the other hand, if one were teaching the geography of rivers, contextualising images might include specific examples of a river mouth, a delta, and a meander. These could be displayed beside each word, making it clear what is being referred to. The decision about whether to use images for broad or specific purposes will depend on your area of study and where you feel your EAL learners are at. Either way, it will help them.

Some words, rules, or phrases are better suited to images, or a collection of images, which demonstrate meaning or the actions which are being requested. If you have class rules, these could be accompanied by images which show them being correctly and incorrectly followed. A series of images could indicate what an abstract word refers to. For example, a circle followed by an arrow followed by a straight line, with the circle and straight line both labelled as the same length. This could demonstrate change, translation, or similarity.

In both the above cases, images are being called upon to help EAL learners deal with more complex language. It can be a creative, challenging experience for the teacher to think up intelligent uses of pictures for language which is conceptual or which is command based. You could even ask your class to help you come up with ideas. This will lead to all of them thinking carefully about language and how to translate its meaning into visual form, while also helping your EAL learners.

As noted, my experience with Turner took me beyond words. You may also be able to use images to achieve this effect with your EAL students. A specific example now follows:

There are certain words which carry specific connotations for most native English speakers. In the United Kingdom 'class' and 'parliament' would be two examples. These words include various histories which children brought up in Britain would most likely be exposed to via the prevailing culture. Using images to supplement words such as these, and explaining them where possible, helps EAL learners to pick up on meanings which we might take granted but that are, in fact, culturally specific and rarely made explicit (certainly in the classroom anyway).

A simple benefit of using images which we have not yet mentioned is as an aid to memorisation. Invoking multiple areas of the brain when learning new information has been shown to aid memory; many specific techniques for enhancing memory are predicated on making visual associations with words or objects. EAL learners will most likely be learning and remembering far more than the rest of your class. Your use of pictures will help them to associate words with images. This should help them to memorise the new language they encounter more easily.

Turning the classroom relationship around, we can also imagine how EAL learners may find images a useful means of communicating with the teacher. By drawing or sketching their thoughts or feelings, students who cannot articulate what they would like to say in speech or writing are in a position to make their ideas clear. While these might lack some of the nuance of that which could be said in language (though it depends somewhat on the artistic abilities of the pupil) they still give the student a 'voice' in the classroom and help them to establish rapport and build a relationship with the teacher.

The final aspect of the use of images which I would draw your attention to is a special case we touched on briefly when thinking about how to demonstrate abstract concepts or rules. It is that of diagrams.

Diagrams can communicate things which are difficult, lengthy, or technical when explained in words. They are an aid to understanding. They can elucidate meaning and simplify language. Their use is a matter of judgement, based on the question: Will they make things clearer for the audience? If the answer is 'yes', then they are well worth using.

I have sketched in outline some of the ways in which pictures and images can assist EAL learners. I have also intimated how you might use them in your teaching resources. The next section will provide eight concrete examples which put into practice the principles and underlying logic of the use of visual media. The topics which I use to exemplify the ideas are purely indicative. All the ideas can be used with subject matter of any type.

1. Pictures for Meaning

Explanation and Rationale

Pictures display meaning which can be decoded by anyone who is familiar with some of the content. They avoid the necessary prior learning which language demands. Any learner can benefit from pictures which signify what is being studied. The pictures act as a supplement to that which is written on the resources and that which is spoken by the teacher. They situate and contextualise the learning. EAL learners can use pictures to access the learning even if they are not yet able to access the language.

Pictures can show the meaning of specific words or situate a topic more broadly. They can be selected so as to call on the prior experience of EAL learners, or they can be deliberately chosen to show something new.

Example One

A lesson looking at the use of genre in writing could make good use of pictures. Appropriate images could be displayed on the board, each one signifying a different genre. These could also serve as a 'way-in' for EAL learners. If they are at an early stage of language development, they could still use the images to write a story in their first language. The likelihood is that the specific differences signified by the pictures will lead them to write in different genres.

Example Two

When introducing a range of new words, produce a worksheet for EAL learners in which each word is accompanied by an illustrative picture. There could be space for students to write in definitions, the equivalent words from their first language, or simple sentences based around each of the new words.

Example Three

Identify certain pictures which you can use repeatedly. For example, if you are studying religious festivals, and the unit looks at a wide variety, you could have the same general image across different lessons. This creates continuity for an EAL learner and makes it clear that what is being taught relates to previous lessons. Another technique is to use images to signify different parts of the lesson, for example the start, middle, and end. This sounds basic, but it can help learners to familiarise themselves with how your lessons are structured and what to expect when and where.

Developments

- Ask EAL learners to draw you pictures of important words in their own language.
- Involve other students by asking them what pictures they think might usefully illustrate ideas or concepts.
- Use a series of images to illustrate a process or the effect one thing can have on something else.

2. Pictures for Class Rules

Explanation and Rationale

Most social situations have rules of some sort, even if these are not stated explicitly. For example, in the United Kingdom it is a generally accepted rule that one queues and waits to be served when in a shop.

Classrooms have rules. They also tend to have consequences for not following the rules. These often take the form of sanctions. If an EAL learner is at an early stage of language development, it will be difficult for them to grasp what the rules are if these are only explained through speech and writing. Using pictures is therefore a good way to help EAL students and to ensure they know what is expected of them. This minimises ambiguity and protects the EAL learner from breaking rules of which they were not fully aware.

Example One

If one of the rules of your classroom is that students ought to be respectful at all times, you could find a couple of suitable pictures to illustrate this point. One could show positive, respectful relationships between two young people, while a second could show the same except with a young person and a teacher. This could be repeated for all your rules.

Example Two

Condense your rules (if necessary) so they fit on an A4 or A5 sheet of paper. Illustrate each rule with a picture. You can give a printed copy to all new students who join the class or, at the beginning of the year, to all your pupils. This ensures that EAL students are supported in understanding the rules but not made to feel distinct from the rest of the class by being given a different document.

Example Three

Rather than having a sheet which you hand out to pupils, you could have your rules displayed in a prominent position in your classroom. Each of these would be accompanied by appropriate pictures in the same way as was outlined in example two. An advantage of having the rules on the wall is that you can refer to them as and when you wish. This could include showing EAL students when other pupils are or are not following them.

Developments

- At the start of the year, ask your students to create the pictures that will illustrate each rule.
- Use two pictures for each rule. One shows the correct behaviour and is accompanied by a tick. The other shows incorrect behaviour and is accompanied by a cross.
- Ask EAL learners to write the rules in their first language, using the pictures as a guide. They could then compare the sentences they have written with the sentences in English.

3. Pictures for Tasks

Explanation and Rationale

Throughout a lesson, students will be asked to engage in a variety of tasks. These may involve quite different behaviours, interactions, and intended outcomes. There are times when a lesson may have multiple transitions and students have to switch between a range of activities, each one with general conventions and conventions specific to you and your classroom. For an EAL learner who is coming to terms with the English language, this has the potential to be confusing.

With any group of students, the change from one activity to another can be ambiguous. Even with clear instructions repeated verbally and made visible on a whiteboard, it is likely that one or two students will need further reassurance or explanation about what is being asked of them. One can assume that EAL learners in the early stages of language development may also struggle to comprehend what the teacher is asking.

The likelihood is that the majority of activities you use in class will fall into a small number of broad categories, for example, discussion, individual writing, and drama. Each of these can be signified by a relevant image. After a couple of examples of the connection between the image and the type of task, students will come to associate the two. The image will then start to signal to them what type of activity is being requested and the expectations which go alongside this.

Example One

Identify a small number of categories into which the activities you tend to use fall. For each of these, find a picture which can act as a signifier. For example, discussion could be signified by an image of an open mouth and a speech bubble; individual writing could be indicated by a picture of someone hunched over a desk, pen in hand; and drama could be represented by the masks of drama (comedy and tragedy). Put these images on your resources whenever you need to signal a change of activity.

Example Two

As you progress through the year, start to group the activities you have in your lessons. To begin, you might choose images to represent the first lot of activities you use with your class. As time goes on, you can assess which new activities can be represented by a picture already in use. This is a method similar to that noted in example one. The difference is that categorisation here is more organic. You judge as you go along, rather than making all the decisions at the start.

Example Three

Choose the images which will represent the different types of activity. Print these onto A4-sized paper. Put these on your classroom wall in a prominent position. When introducing a new activity, point to the appropriate poster to indicate the association. An advantage of this method is that you can also include a written description of what is expected of students beneath each poster.

4. Draw Your Answer

Explanation and Rationale

We have observed that visual media can transcend language. Two individuals who cannot communicate by speaking or writing can nonetheless use images to convey meaning to one another. This principle extends to one of those people using drawing to display what it is they are thinking but which they do not have the shared language to say.

I am not able to speak Italian, nor can I understand the spoken or written Italian of others. Yet, when I look at the paintings of Caravaggio I *can* grasp some (perhaps much) of the latent meaning. I can deduce and infer, compare and contrast, look for similarities and identify examples of general cases. All of this is despite me not sharing a language with the artist and, for that matter, the fact that he was born and died centuries before me.

EAL learners can use drawing as a means to convey their understanding. It can be a bridge across the divide or a supplement to aid burgeoning interactions in English. It is also a means to ensure everyone in the class can provide an answer to a question, regardless of the stage of their language development. Granted, an EAL learner may not be able to understand the question posed; looking at the drawings of their peers will help them though.

Example One

Set a starter or plenary which asks for a drawn answer. This could involve students using mini-whiteboards or sketching something in their books. One way to go about this is to set a question and then model the approach yourself: draw your own answer on the whiteboard and ask students to follow suit.

Example Two

For a student whose speaking and listening is ahead of their reading and writing, pictures can help bridge the gap and minimise frustration. Ask an EAL learner to write some simple sentences (or even just the key words they think are relevant) and to supplement this with more detailed drawings. Detail here could mean more content within a single image or the display of change or causation through a sequence of images.

Example Three

If a student is at the earliest stages of English language development, find out how to write a few of the key words appropriate to your lesson in the student's first language. Give these to the pupil and ask them to draw all the things which they associate with those words. You could start them off by modelling one or two examples. Once the student has finished, ask them to look up the English translations for their drawings in a bilingual dictionary. Such an activity involves the pupil in the lesson while taking account of their current abilities.

5. Mini-Whiteboards

Explanation and Rationale

We have touched on some of the uses of mini-whiteboards. In the case of EAL learners, perhaps the greatest benefit is their provisional nature. Writing done on a whiteboard, unlike the majority of writing produced in a classroom, can be swiftly erased. What is more, little or no trace ever remains. Not only does this provide space for experimentation, it also makes it easier to take risks and to deal with mistakes.

For many of us, erring in public can feel embarrassing or, at worst, humiliating. The shame or awkwardness that may come to be associated with it – regardless of whether this has any rational basis – has the capacity to stymie people's efforts to learn new things or to take risks in order to try to achieve their goals.

It is no different for students. In fact, for EAL learners the situation may even be compounded. Aware of the relative skill with which those around them manipulate the English language, some pupils may feel that their own developing abilities could draw derision or ridicule. While we all strive to create a safe, positive atmosphere in our classrooms, there can still be times when EAL learners feel uncomfortable. Using mini-whiteboards is one way to remove the perceived permanence of writing and the public nature of speaking.

Example One

Give mini-whiteboards to EAL students and encourage them to use these in your lessons. Explain they can use them to practise their writing before committing anything to paper. Tell them to indicate if they would like their writing on the whiteboard checked before they write it up. You might develop this technique by pairing EAL learners with a friend or a sensitive peer who can help them to check the writing themselves.

Example Two

Give students mini-whiteboards when you are doing discussion activities. Explain that these should be used for rehearsing answers or for making notes which will help the student when they come to speak. You might also suggest that pupils write their thoughts on their whiteboards and share these, with the discussion growing out of what they have written.

Example Three

Give EAL learners mini-whiteboards to use in your lessons. Ask them to look up new words they come across in a dictionary and to draw these on their whiteboards. You can then discuss meanings and definitions with the students, using the images as a starting point. Similarly, you might encourage EAL students to write out definitions, or sentences involving key words, on their whiteboards for you to check and to then discuss with them.

6. Matching and Grid Activities

Explanation and Rationale

Language is built on connections. When learning a new word, one must learn its meaning. The connection between physical sound and mental association is inherent. If a newcomer to English were taught how to speak a series of words with great accuracy they would remain, nonetheless, completely inept at communication unless they were also taught the meaning of these words (and, therefore, of the sounds).

Language is a representation of things 'out there' in the physical world and things which are known only to ourselves (like, for example, the feeling of toothache. While other people tell us they also get toothache, they do not get 'our' toothache. We have to tell them when we have it). With the first category, we assume that one and all share in them and that this is demonstrable because the world is as it is, interactions with it can be tested and repeated, and we mostly provide similar accounts of it (we would not believe someone who said they could crush rocks like they could crush paper). The second category is a little more complex and involves the development of introspection and the articulation of what is inside one's own mind (and body).

Regardless of which category a word falls into, its meaning must be learnt in conjunction with its sound and, quite likely, its spelling. Students will need to be able to identify relationships between words and meanings. Matching and grid activities provide a useful way to help them do this.

Example One

When teaching new vocabulary, provide EAL students with a sheet containing the new words alongside a series of pictures which represent the meaning of each word. Jumble the pictures so they are not next to the word with which they correspond. Ask students to match the pictures to the correct words. After they have done this, discuss how they went about making their choices and what meanings the different pictures represented.

Example Two

Create a grid with three columns: word, meaning, image. Choose a series of words you want your EAL learners to focus on. For each word, complete one of the columns. Ask your students to fill in the gaps. You can alter the activity to make it easier or more difficult. To make it easier, complete two of the columns for some of the words. To make it harder, add a fourth column titled 'Example of a Sentence Containing the Word'.

Example Three

Give students a series of images. Ask them to match these to the correct word in their first language. Next, ask the pupils to use a bilingual dictionary to look up the English equivalents of these words. They should then create a mini-glossary encompassing pictures, the English words, and the first-language equivalents. The activity involves two stages of matching. The latter builds on the existing knowledge exhibited in the first.

7. Culturally Relevant Pictures

Explanation and Rationale

Language is dependent on context. This relationship can take many forms. For example:

1. A specific word that has multiple meanings. Toast is an example: 'Can I have some toast?'; 'I propose a toast'; 'He was the toast of the town'.
2. Words which gain or lose power depending on who says them. Compare a neighbour and a judge saying: 'This is the last time'.
3. Phrases which rely on intonation and the situation in which they are said. Consider how, 'Is that it?' could vary in meaning.

Another key aspect in the contextualisation of language is culture. The word 'restaurant' may have different connotations for a French person and an English person. Even within a culture, understanding is likely to differ. The spoken word 'bread' may mean money and sandwiches to one person, breakfast and lineage to another (as in the homophone 'bred'). And meanings shift over time. Rake, as in reprobate, is now considered archaic. Yet at one time it was the norm.

Being alive to context and the influence of culture is important. There are a number of ways in which this might help you when working with EAL learners. One of these is using culturally relevant pictures. Here you will be playing on the cultural connotations students have developed in their first language. These can be a shortcut helping learners to access the meaning of corresponding words in English. It may require a bit of research on your part (unless you or a colleague have an existing knowledge of your student's culture), but this will be easily offset by the assistance it brings, as well as the rapport it will help to create.

Example One

Use a mixture of images on your resources. Draw some from your usual sources and some from cultural sources with which your EAL learners may already be familiar. For example, if you are studying heroes as part of a literacy unit of work, and you have EAL learners who are Hindu in your class, you could incorporate pictures of Krishna or Rama. This will help students to situate the concept of heroes and to connect the word 'hero', as it is written and as it is said, to the mental concept they already possess.

Example Two

Give students a list of words in English. Ask them to translate these into their first language using a bilingual dictionary. Once they have done this, ask them to connect each word to a picture they are familiar with. The images could be drawn, cut out of magazines, or printed from the internet. This task makes use of students' existing understanding to help them grasp new words in English. The pictures they are familiar with will begin to be connected to the English words through the course of the activity.

8. Diagrams

Explanation and Rationale

Diagrams have a number of uses. Some of these include:

- To demonstrate a process or relationship.
- To exemplify something conveyed in writing or speech.
- To simplify complex ideas.
- To show change over time.
- To represent something in the world (usually schematically).

Common to all these is the process of visualisation. This may be in place of the written or spoken word, or it might be in addition to it. Either way, the author is creating a display of something which is in their mind or something which is out in the world (although it still goes through their mind. After all, they have to perceive it prior to turning it into a diagram).

Diagrams have the capacity to transcend language. To do this, though, the shapes and symbols of which they are made up must be understandable. For example, most GCSE science students will be able to correctly identify a diagram of an electrical circuit. Many will also be able to indicate to what each part refers. However, a child who has never encountered the concept of circuits will struggle to decode the diagram.

This sounds an obvious point. It is important to remember though that while diagrams generally simplify (by expressing things more quickly than could be managed in words), that does not preclude the possibility that they may confuse or befuddle. We may take the case of public toilets as an example. While a great many people the world over may be able to decode silhouetted images of a man and a woman stuck to separate doors, they would still require the prior knowledge that such a sign indicates male and female *toilets*. Without this, their understanding of the diagrams is severely limited.

Remember then, while diagrams are an excellent aid to communication, they must still be used with care. You will have to assess whether they rely on prior knowledge and, if they do, whether your EAL learners possess this or not.

Example One

Use diagrams on your resources to specify what it is you want students to do. An example would be a picture of a student, followed by an arrow, followed by a pen. This suggests that students should be writing with their pens for the current task. Another example would be to have two separate pictures, both of students, set slightly apart. Coming from each of these would be an arrow, angling in at forty-five degrees. Where these arrows join, there would be a picture of two students working together. The diagram indicates pupils should move to work in pairs.

Example Two

Give EAL learners diagrams to help explain certain concepts. These should help clarify the meaning of the words for students. You will have to identify what concepts are amenable to this method; those which involve change or processes, for example.

CHAPTER FOUR

The Teacher

There is much any teacher can do to help students who are learning English as an additional language. This chapter contains a range of strategies, techniques, and activities in which the teacher – what they do and how they go about doing it – is central. Before we get onto those, let us think about the teacher, language, and classroom.

In almost every lesson the teacher will be the most highly skilled practitioner in the language of instruction (an exception would be a non-native languages teacher who has a linguistically mature native speaker in their class).

This position of unparalleled proficiency is usually taken for granted. It is assumed to be the case because in education those who know instruct those who do not. Our education system centres on young people. Therefore, those who know will by necessity be older than those who do not. They will also have passed certain examinations which are an entry requirement for the profession. A person (or persons) already in employment and with obligations to the institution will have given them their job.

The teacher will thus have had more time using the language of instruction than their students. They will have used it at a higher level. The results of this will have been sufficiently good to ensure they are able to become a teacher. People morally bound by a duty to others will have assessed their proficiency. Procedures will be in place to remove the teacher if they have deceived in regard to their capabilities.

In the teacher's (near) inevitable linguistic ascendancy over their students – this most obvious of facts – there lies a wealth of potential. As the height of linguistic sophistication in the classroom, teachers become models for their students. Everything they do concerning language and communication can aid the pupils' development. They provide a case study in how an adult, living and working in society, makes use of language in order to interact with others and to achieve certain ends. This is a powerful, and useful, position to be in.

Being aware of it ought to cause the teacher to reflect on how they use language, as well as other means of communication such as gestures, in their classroom. If we know that we are modelling language use for our students, we ought to be alive to precisely what it is that we are modelling. Are we using slang? Are we listening actively to what our students say? Do we ask questions of clarification? Do we adjust our language to ensure we make ourselves understood? How carefully do we consider what we say, before we say it?

Such questions ought not to stymie our interactions with pupils. Trying to model good language skills would be pointless if it entailed communicating in an unnatural, stilted fashion. Rather, we should seek to keep the power of our position at the forefront of our minds, avoiding the trap of forgetting about it amid its seeming ordinariness.

The most common means by which a teacher is aware of their role as a model is when they are showing students what they want them to do. This 'modelling' is common to good teaching. It diminishes ambiguity by providing a visual display of what the teacher has asked for through speech or writing. An example which sticks clearly in my mind comes from when I was at school. Each Christmas, PE lessons were given over for a few weeks to ballroom dancing. At the start of the sessions, one of our teachers would grab hold of a partner and perform an exaggerated version of the steps we were supposed to be learning. This contextualised the spoken explanation he had previously given, providing a visual reference through which each of us could know for certain what it was he meant. It avoided ambiguity and was no doubt performed with the intention of getting us all off and going, the teenage psyche being rather less than obliging in such settings.

Using your body to model what it is you want students to do is help-ful. Gestures can also reinforce praise and disapproval or magnify your reactions so as to make it clear to students you are taking what they say seriously. This must not fall into the realm of farce, because then your actions lose any impact, perhaps even offending students who do not be-lieve you are being genuine. The classroom *is* a theatrical space, though – think about how drama can be whipped up by things which elsewhere would be innocuous at best. Finding ways in which to use this theatri-cality can help you to critically consider your role as teacher in relation to language and communication.

We looked in detail at speaking and listening in the last chapter. Let us return to it here, albeit briefly, in the context of modelling. As we noted earlier, speaking and listening are integral to most people's everyday lives. This includes our students and their lives. We also observed that there is a clear distinction between the purposes of speaking and listening in the classroom and the purposes which may hold in other settings.

It can be difficult to convey this to students, not least because of the amount of speaking and listening they will likely be involved in outside of school. That which takes place in the classroom will be the anomaly, not the other way round.

Modelling the kind of speaking and listening which you expect of students is one of the most effective ways to ensure it is forthcoming. Demonstrating how you want your students to listen to one another and how you want them to speak to one another, through the speaking and listening you do with them, is a clear way of making your expectations known. It diminishes ambiguity regarding what those expectations ought to look like in practice and provides you with a contrast to use if a student is not doing what you have asked of them.

You may wish to draw attention to exactly what it is you do when you listen to students or when you speak to them. For example, you may talk about what your body and face are doing, how you are attending to their thoughts, or the processes you are going through prior to speaking. This 'making explicit' can give students specific practices to grab hold of and integrate into their own speaking and listening.

The alternative is to leave things implicit. Opting for this method, you will be expecting students to fall into step with the ways of acting you repeatedly demonstrate. The advantage is that such a method can feel more natural and can encounter less resistance. The implied message is: 'This is how we are doing things, and I expect you will do the same.' On the down side, it may be that certain students will not necessarily pick up on this message. This has the potential to create conflict, and you would do well to be alive to this possibility in advance. Assess your classes before deciding what approach to take. And be ready to adapt if the need arises.

This leads us on to a consideration of flexibility more widely. It is an asset in teaching in general and is especially beneficial when teaching EAL learners.

Language development is an uneven process. It does not progress smoothly, and nor will its constituents (reading, writing, speaking, and listening) develop at the same rate. Working with EAL learners, you will need to regularly assess where their development is at, as well as the relative level of development they display in each of the four areas. This information can be used to adapt the tasks and activities in your lessons in order to meet their needs.

In many cases, teachers find themselves teaching a class in which a small number of students have English as an additional language. In such settings, it is likely that those students will be receiving targeted one-to-one or small-group support during the week, to help them develop their English-language skills. As such, the skills they bring to the teacher's classroom will be changing lesson by lesson. Some weeks may see significant progress; other weeks may be slow going. Either way, the students' ability level will not remain static.

Being flexible in how you teach and the activities you use is thus of utmost importance. If students are arriving at your lesson with a level of skill which is roughly, but not precisely, known, then you ought to plan with this in mind. Think in advance about how you might differentiate tasks to accommodate the changing skill levels of EAL learners. Have strategies in this book on hand ready to use. Supplement your main planning with personalised planning predicated on a careful consideration of where the students' language skills might be at, based on what you know they can do already.

If you are lucky enough to have staff in your school whose job it is to work with EAL students full time, then you are in a good position. Search out these staff members and talk to them about the students. They will know a great deal about their characters, background, and the progress they have made since starting at your school. This information is likely to be more accurate and more extensive than that which you will have been able to gather because of the greater time these staff members will have spent with the students.

As well as finding out more about your EAL learners from these colleagues, you will be able to discover more about language development too. The insights you gain from conversations on the topic will further help in your quest to do the best for your EAL learners. It may be that you find out more activities or strategies to use or that you gain a better understanding of what language development looks like on a day-to-day basis. If you have the time, ask to go in and observe the teaching that goes on. Not only will this help you get a sense of what the students are doing during the week, but it will also suggest to those students that you are interested in them and the lives they lead in school outside of your classroom.

If you yourself are an EAL specialist in your school, or if your school does not have an EAL specialist, then go beyond your immediate boundaries and search out expertise elsewhere. Find out if your Local Authority employs EAL staff and whether you can arrange a time to meet them and pick their brains. If this is not possible, look at other schools in your surrounding area. Should this prove unworkable as well, identify areas of the country which you know to have high migrant populations (these are usually large urban centres). It is likely that schools in these areas will have a higher proportion of EAL learners. If you do not work in one already, get in touch and see if they can offer you any advice or help. Finally, NALDIC – the National Association for Language Development in the Curriculum – have an excellent website containing a wide range of useful resources. At the time of writing, the website address is www. naldic.org.uk.

The message here is simple. As a teacher working with EAL students, you are not alone. Seek out help and support, whether it is through this book, through colleagues in school, or through going further afield. Whichever method you choose will be of benefit, both to you and to your EAL learners. If you feel uncertain about what to ask when you go to others for advice, just be honest. Tell them where you are at with your students and where you would like to get to. Ask them if they can help you to close the gap.

Another group you should talk to about teaching your EAL learners is the learners themselves. This will be dependent to some extent on the stage of language development they are at. Clearly it will be difficult to speak about teaching and learning if your students are at the earliest stages of learning English. A situation such as this is not insurmountable, though. If you can get hold of an interpreter, then they can assist you in trying to find out what is working and what is not working in your lessons for your EAL learners. Ask around your school to see whether anyone is fluent in the first language you are looking for. Alternatively, see if there are any parents who can speak the first language as well as English.

Whichever way you come to it, talking to EAL learners about your lessons can provide invaluable information that it would be otherwise difficult to get hold of. Learners will be able to give you feedback on what you have been doing and tell you whether or not they feel it is working. Also, they may be able to pick out specific areas where they are having difficulties or indicate what they are finding easy. Knowing this will allow you to better plan how to support them or to take advantage of their existing strengths.

Having considered some aspects of the teacher's role in the classroom and how this connects to teaching EAL students, let us now look at specific strategies, techniques, and activities which you can build into your lessons.

1. Preteach Vocabulary

Explanation and Rationale

One needs to know what something is before being able to use it. When working with something for the first time, the steps with which one begins are often tentative. This is because there is a lack of knowledge about the extents and capacities of what is being dealt with. The first steps have a dual purpose. On the one hand, they are an attempt to assimilate information about the thing in question. On the other hand, they represent an investigation of what that thing can do and how it ought to be used. As more time is spent with the thing in question, so the ability to manipulate it improves, along with an understanding of the thing's nature.

Let us illustrate this with an example. We meet a word for the first time. The word is 'envelope'. Immediately, we are trying to assimilate the following information: what the word looks like, what the word sounds like, how the word is spelt, how the spelling connects (or not) to the sound, what the word means. As we engage in this process, we are also beginning to ask what the word can do. Questions need to be answered. They may be of the order: To what does this word refer (here there is overlap with assimilating knowledge of its meaning)? Where can this word be used? How can this word be used? What type of word is this? The list could go on.

EAL learners will go through this dual process more often than students who already have highly developed English-language skills. It is time-consuming and often difficult. This is compounded by the fact that in a lesson, we are usually asking students to do things with words which are well beyond these tentative first steps (as we assume that most students will be past this stage). Preteaching vocabulary is a way in which the teacher can mitigate any problems arising from the different stages which EAL learners are at compared to their peers. It takes the students past those first steps, giving them time in which to get to grips with words, so that they can engage in activities with other pupils on a more even footing.

Example One

If you have another adult working with you in the classroom, such as a learning support assistant or a student teacher, ask them to spend some time teaching EAL learners key pieces of vocabulary that you know you will be using in future lessons. This does mean that those learners will be taken away from the present activities. The long-term benefits of such a method should easily outweigh anything which is lost in the short run, however.

Example Two

Identify an aspect of the lesson which will be difficult for EAL learners to access. This could entail choosing an activity which you feel they could do but for which their language skills are not yet sufficiently developed to allow them to get a lot out of it. While the rest of the class complete the activity, you can work with your EAL learners, teaching them vocabulary which will be useful in future lessons. It is a case of weighing up the alternatives. Ask yourself whether the students will benefit more from the planned activity or from learning vocabulary which they will get a chance to put into practice in later lessons.

Example Three

Find a way of teaching EAL learners new vocabulary outside of your lessons. This might involve giving them a list of words in English and asking them to look up the equivalents in their first language for homework. It could see you giving a list of key vocabulary to a specialist EAL teacher who works with the students during the week and asking them to include these words in the lessons they teach. Or, it could be that you set aside some time during the week to work with your EAL learners outside of lessons. This last option will be less onerous if you limit it to one focussed session near the beginning of each term. This will give you the opportunity to preteach all the key words you know will be relevant in the weeks to follow.

2. Questioning

Explanation and Rationale

Teachers ask thousands of questions every week. Students try to provide the answers. The teacher is in a position to direct these answers through the way in which they frame their questions. It is generally for the teacher to decide what the questions will be. It is therefore also for them to decide how the questions will be structured.

A simple example of this with which most people are familiar is the difference between open and closed questions. Open questions invite an extended response; they give the person answering space in which to speak or write: What are your thoughts on this? How might we solve the problem? Closed questions, on the other hand, restrict the possible answers which might be given; they narrow the field down, usually to just a couple of options: Are you coming out tonight, or not? What is the capital of France?

Given that we use questions so extensively, we ought to think carefully about how we are using them. When teaching students for whom English is an additional language, we can tailor our questions to take account of their particular needs. By doing this, we are able to use questioning in such a way that it supports those learners, allowing them to experience success in the classroom and to communicate their thoughts and ideas.

Example One

Open questions are better than closed questions in most situations. They give students the opportunity to share their thoughts with you rather than having to find (or guess) a specific answer which is deemed to be correct. Of course, there are times when closed questions are necessary and useful, but even in these situations the approach is used at the expense of elaboration.

By asking open questions you can show EAL learners that you are not searching for a 'right' answer. Instead, you are seeking to find out what they think. In so doing, you will be able to assess what students know, as well as the way in which they know it (as open questions will generally require reasoning of some kind to support the answer given). Using open questions is thus good for the learner, as it removes the anxiety which can be associated with having to find the 'one' answer, and good for the teacher because it provides detailed information which can be used to accurately assess student learning.

Example Two

In the Introduction we noted that EAL learners are, in many ways, just the same as other students and that the key difference is in the point on the continuum of language development at which they find themselves. Using these two premises – of similarity and difference – we can develop questioning which is closely tied to the needs of EAL learners. Differentiated questioning in this sense involves the subject of the questioning remaining the same, but the structure and the demands of the questioning being made simpler.

For example: 'In what ways does the text convey emotion?' could become: 'How does this make you feel?' with the follow-up question being 'Why?' This could then be followed by a question such as: 'Which bits make you feel like that? Can you point to them?' We could continue: 'What happens in those bits? Are they the same?' and so on.

There are two points to note. First, one can achieve similar ends through different questions. Second, differentiated questioning may involve asking a series of questions rather than just the one. This means the learner is being asked to take a series of little steps. The accumulated thinking this elicits will help them get close to what the rest of the class is doing. It allows you and the learner to build understanding gradually.

Each step comes on top of the thinking which has gone before. This makes the process easier and simpler.

3. Learning Support

Explanation and Rationale

Learning support assistants (LSAs), also known as Teaching Assistants (although some schools may employ people as both and differentiate the job roles), work in classrooms under the direction of a teacher. They are usually attached either to a particular student or to a particular class. They may have certain specialisms, such as working with students who are on the autism spectrum. The quickest way to find out what experience an LSA has and which students in your school they work with is to talk to them, ideally outside of lesson time.

If you have an LSA attached to your class who has experience working with EAL students, then you are in a great position. They may well know more about the subject in general, or the students in particular, than you do. If so, make as much of this opportunity as possible. Ask them for their ideas and suggestions, plan activities for your EAL learners with them, observe how they work with the students and what they do to help them learn. It may be that the best approach you can take is to ask them to work closely with your EAL learners and to keep you informed of their progress. You will need to judge how beneficial your own input will be.

If the LSA who is attached to your class does not have experience with EAL learners, there are still ways in which you can work with them to the benefit of those students. The key thing to remember is that an LSA is a second skilled adult working in your room. This means there is scope to do things which would not be possible if you were in there on your own. Work can be divided between the two of you, students or small groups can spend exclusive time with either you or the LSA, and specific areas of language development can be focussed on. These three ideas are developed below.

Example One

Ask your LSA to take a section of the lesson. This could be the starter, a single activity, or the plenary. It is important to be certain that your LSA feels comfortable doing this and that they are at ease with leading the whole class. If they are not comfortable, then that must be accepted and the matter brought to an end. Let us assume, however, that they are OK with it. While they are working with the rest of the class, you can devote your complete attention to some, or all, of your EAL learners. This will allow you to get a detailed sense of where they are at in relation to the topic and to gauge the current level of their English language abilities. It will also give you a chance to do specific activities with them, perhaps different from what the rest of the students are doing.

Example Two

Explain to your LSA that you would like them to work exclusively with one EAL student, or a small group of EAL learners. Devise some differentiated tasks you would like the LSA to lead and explain to them that the focus is on developing students' language skills while also ensuring they access the work in which the whole class is engaged. If possible, spend some time talking with your LSA about how to support EAL learners. Discuss some of the strategies and techniques which can be used to achieve this.

Example Three

You may find yourself working with EAL learners for whom one specific aspect of the English language proves particularly difficult. This could be one of the broad areas we used to define language earlier – reading, writing, speaking, and listening – or it could be something more specific, such as writing formally or reading academic texts. If you have an LSA in your classroom, you can ask them to work with your EAL learner, focussing specifically on whatever has been identified as the major difficulty. This may result in them going off topic for a lesson or two. So be it. The judgement is yours to make. You will need to decide whether an intensive period working strictly on an area of weakness will bring benefits which outweigh missing a small amount of content. I would suggest that in most cases it will.

4. Thinking Time

Explanation and Rationale

Good thinking takes time. Although some decisions can be made in an instant, with many of these leading to good results, it is questionable whether the individual involved in such a decision could say truthfully that they thought about what they were doing. It is more likely they followed their instincts or went with their gut (as the sayings go). Often, such a process is apt. In some circumstances too much thinking could be hugely detrimental, for example, when deciding whether to pass or shoot in a football match. There are many other situations we could point to where taking time to think can also impede one's chance of success.

The classroom is not one of these places, however. Here we are more concerned with the thinking students do than the swiftness with which they make decisions. Answers to questions which are shot back at rapid speed are unlikely to be much good. It is not just the student who can go too quickly, though. A teacher who fires off question after question, or who demands answers as soon as a question has been posed, is facilitating a dynamic in which the importance of thinking is diminished and the immediate is favoured ahead of the good.

EAL learners are particularly vulnerable to quick-fire questioning from a teacher who is demanding answers. All students benefit from being given time to think, time in which to formulate a response. EAL learners, for whom English is a map still unfolding, will be less capable than their peers of answering quickly. They will have to consider both the content and the form of the question being asked, what the individual words mean and what they mean together (including the kind of response being requested). Giving all students thinking time is a laudable acknowledgement of the importance of thinking and the primacy of reflection over haste. It will aid EAL learners and take away some of the fear which the demand for immediate answers can engender.

Example One

When you are asking a question, whether it be to the whole class, an individual, or a group, tell students to think about their answers before they reply. You may like to give them a specific time frame: 'OK, thirty seconds thinking time and then we will hear some answers.' Explain to students why you are doing this and the importance of thinking and reflecting on questions before giving an answer.

Example Two

When you are working with EAL learners, be mindful of the need not to rush them. Study the speed at which you are talking and the expectations of pace you bring to the conversation. Keep a check on both of these, and, if appropriate, slow down. Maintain an open posture and an inquiring look (though not such that it looks forced) so as to convey the fact that you want to know what pupils think and are happy to wait to find out.

Example Three

If you are running a discussion activity, ask students to make some brief notes before they do any speaking. This has three benefits. First, it slows pupils down by giving them an extra process to go through. Second, writing entails a degree of synthesis. This takes time because students are reflecting on their thoughts – refining, clarifying, and rearranging what is in their head so as to transfer it onto paper. Third, EAL learners specifically will benefit because it gives them extra opportunities to practise the translation from thinking and speaking to writing.

5. Belonging

Explanation and Rationale

Psychologists have long known the importance a sense of belonging has for people. The knowledge predates their study of human thought and behaviour, though they have articulated it in a scientific form. We are animal organisms with certain needs which have to be met in order for us to feel at ease. These go from the mundane – food, heat, and water – to the profound – love and self-expression. If we find ourselves in a situation where many of our needs are met, we develop a sense of belonging, a secure attachment to that place.

Philosophers have known longer than psychologists that this is the way of things. In Ancient Greece the question of how one should live in order to be happy and content was debated at length, both in oral discussion and in writing. Analyses were made of the nature of man (today we would add 'and woman') in which thinkers sought to identify various different elements which go to make up human beings. They also sought to apply their findings, giving direction to others on how best to live so that life was good. Their aim was to identify how one might come to flourish in the ways that one would wish.

We do not have time to hold forth to students about the right way to live. There are, after all, lessons to be taught. What we can do, though, is take these ideas about belonging and the identification of what goes to make a good life and apply them to our classrooms. EAL learners in particular are likely to feel discomfort in school. A sense of alienation can develop if they are at an early stage of language development. Frustration, fear, and anger may also make themselves known. Unfortunately there is also the chance of bullying or cold-shouldering by their peers. Children, just like adults, have the capacity to identify and reject difference. The activities which follow all work to help create a sense of belonging in the classroom, supporting EAL students in the process.

Example One

Celebrate diversity. As the teacher, you are the professional who leads and directs the class. While they are with you, your rules are their rules and your standards are what they have to live up to. By celebrating diversity you can use this position of power to highlight difference in a positive sense. You could ask students to bring things in to show and tell, each of which should be in some way representative of their background. You could do some work around identity and diversity, exploring students' family histories. Finally, you could ask pupils to write biographies of themselves which they then take it in turns to share. All these activities are predicated on seeing difference positively. They will all help to increase students' knowledge and understanding of one another.

Example Two

Create a support network for EAL students. We touched on this idea earlier when we spoke about buddying EAL learners with native English speakers. The idea can be further developed by having a collection of students whom, you ask to support EAL learners. Taking this on further still, you can set up a school-wide support network. This might involve meetings for EAL learners who want to share their experiences, language exchange classes out of lesson time, culture swaps, a clear indication to EAL learners which staff speak which languages, and so on.

Example Three

Celebrate linguistic diversity. If you have EAL learners in your class, then your class has linguistic diversity. Make use of this fact and celebrate it. You could ask learners who can speak another language to teach the rest of the class (including yourself) a few words or phrases. You could run an activity in which students take part in a language exchange. This involves each student indicating what languages they can speak and pairs or groups getting together to swap words and phrases. Finally, you could ask EAL learners to make a presentation to the class about their first language and, if appropriate, the country in which they learnt to speak it and the culture which exists there.

6. Eliciting Prior Knowledge
Explanation and Rationale

Every student arrives at every lesson with a wealth of experience, knowledge, and understanding. The difficulty for teachers is twofold. First, trying to gauge what exactly each student knows and how they know it, and second, helping students to build on this. It is always worth the effort. Learning is like constructing a house. You must be sure the foundations are there first so that later trouble is avoided. It is also like catching fish. If you can hook students with something they are already familiar with, then you've got them!

In any situation, it is better to elicit prior knowledge than to plough on regardless. Things are no different when working with EAL learners. Pupils who are developing their abilities in English are just as likely to have a wide range of knowledge, experience, and understanding as anyone else. This might be more difficult for them to convey – or for you to elicit – because of the potential language barriers, but it can still be drawn out and used to help both the student and the teacher.

Even having said that, there are specific areas of the curriculum about which students learning English as an additional language may know little, or even next to nothing. An example would be a student who has moved between countries and is near the beginning of the language development continuum. It is unlikely that such a pupil would have encountered the history of the English-speaking country in which they are living. They may know a great deal about the history of the country from which they have come, but perhaps not a lot about the history of their new country. Ascertaining unfamiliarity is as important as discovering understanding. In both cases you are gaining information which can be used to help the student.

Example One

When starting a new topic, ask pupils to make a spider diagram which contains everything they can think of relating to a relevant key word. When they have done this, ask them to explain their spider diagrams to one another, before sharing their ideas with the whole class. If students are not able to read or write English, provide them with a picture instead of a key word. Model a spider diagram around this picture. You could use images instead of words or words written in the student's first language.

Example Two

If you have a member of staff, or an older student, in school who can speak the first language of your EAL learner, ask them to have a discussion with the pupil about what they have previously studied. This need not take a great deal of time and could be conducted using a set of questions you develop. Once the discussion is over (and you might want to sit in on it), the translator can explain what the student has said. This process will help you picture more accurately in your own mind what the EAL learner's prior schooling was like.

Example Three

Use assessment for learning techniques to elicit information from students about what they already know. This could include setting up discussion tasks to which you listen in, providing pieces of paper on which students write what they already know about a topic, or setting a test at the start of a new unit. You may need to modify your chosen techniques to take account of the specific requirements of your EAL learners, but the logic underpinning the activities will remain the same.

7. Analogies

Explanation and Rationale

Analogies are a means of reasoning. They make claims by comparing two or more things (though usually two) in order to demonstrate similarity. The inference is that the similarity which is shown extends to the thing in question more widely. This gives insight into what it is and how it should be classed as well as more specific elements such as its structure or specific features. The latter will be dependent upon the particular analogy.

In effect, an analogy is reasoning of the order: A is similar to B. Therefore, there is reason to treat A in accordance with how we treat B.

The reason is dependent upon the audience's acceptance of the validity of the analogy. They will need to look at the claim of similarity and assess whether they agree with it. They will also need to consider whether the analogy is suitably apt – whether it fits sufficiently – for the claims it makes about A to be accepted.

Analogies are useful because they convey meaning in a different sense to formal reasoning or detailed explanation. They have a visual element to them, make use of existing knowledge, and play on our abilities to recognise patterns (specifically, patterns of similarities). They can help one explain complex ideas quickly and easily. The explanation may not be total, but it will usually be sufficient for the speaker's purposes.

When working with EAL learners, it can be helpful to use analogies. You will need to be certain that students are familiar with 'B' already (that to which you compare the new idea). If they are not, you will need to alter the analogy or do away with it altogether.

The greatest benefit comes from the leap in understanding which analogies can facilitate. Because they rely upon the prior knowledge of the audience, they to some extent circumvent the more elaborate, and sometimes tortuous, expositions which are often associated with complex or unusual ideas. In addition, they can articulate clearly and precisely things which are difficult to formulate simply through extended speech or writing. An example would be the meaning of an abstract concept or the relationship between two distinct processes. In both cases it is likely that with concerted effort a simple verbal or written explanation could be arrived at, but this will take time over and above that available to the teacher who is working in the classroom.

Analogies do the work of many words and can act as a booster to understanding for EAL learners. A couple of examples ought to point the way:

♦ In Sociology, Functionalists see society as being like a human body. The different sections – education, the family, the police, and so on – are like the organs. All work together and complement each other. This means the whole system runs smoothly. If one thing breaks down, it affects the whole structure.

The analogy here is that, for Functionalists, society is like the human body. The analogy fits because society, like the human body, is made up of many different parts, each of which is important and each of which has its own function to perform. Equally, in both society and the human body, if one part breaks down there are consequences for the rest of the system.

- The road network in the United Kingdom is like the circulatory system in human beings. In both, a collection of differently sized channels allow bodies to reach their destinations.

Again we have an analogy with part of the human body. The advantage of this is that everyone has experience of the human body. Therefore it is almost guaranteed that any audience will be able to understand the analogy. Here, the fit is again good. There are a sequence of similarities: the differently sized channels (arteries, veins, and capillaries: motorways, 'A' roads and 'B' roads); conveyance of bodies along the channels (blood cells: motor vehicles); a series of destinations served by the channels, to which the bodies travel (organs, muscles, tissue: cities, towns, villages). These various points combine to create a stronger case for the analogy being accepted.

As noted, you will need to think carefully about the analogies you use with EAL learners, ensuring that the things compared are things with which they are familiar. The benefits of using analogies are great. They can help students developing their understanding of English to make great strides. The potential risks are minimal. If you make a bad analogy or your students do not get the analogy, you simply move on and try again.

8. Idioms
Explanation and Rationale
Here are five idioms:

- It's raining cats and dogs.
- He's a man of the cloth.
- She's got a hat-trick!
- Don't sail close to the wind.
- They really saved my bacon.

And here are literal translations of these:

- Cats and dogs are falling to earth from out of the clouds.
- He is either made of cloth or he works in the textile industry, perhaps selling cloth.
- She has a trick of some sort involving a hat.
- If you are in a boat, avoid getting close to the wind. This would seem to be very difficult. One would need to know where all the wind was in advance. It would also be difficult to sail without

any wind. A motor would be required on the boat, but this would mean it was false to say 'don't sail'.

♦ The person had some bacon which was in danger, and these other people saved it. Quite what endangered the bacon is not made clear.

Do not use idioms when working with EAL learners. They are confusing. They are illogical. Invariably, there is no obvious connection between the words which go to make up the idiom and the meaning which that idiom possesses.

There are idiom dictionaries available which explain the historical origins of these types of phrases. When native English speakers learn them, it is usually through hearing them used in context. It may take many hearings before the speaker understands what the meaning is and can use the idiom correctly. It is likely that at no point will they be made aware of the actual origin of the phrase. Their knowledge of it will be through experience of its use and therefore of its meaning.

EAL learners, once they have developed a good degree of fluency in English, may well learn some or many idioms. They are not exclusively for native speakers, not by any means. No matter where your EAL students are at on the continuum, though, it is better to avoid using idioms in the classroom. They will do little other than confuse matters, placing the learners on the back foot (idiom) and opening up a can of worms (idiom). Dodge the bullet (idiom), and avoid your lessons going pear-shaped (you get the idea). Do not use idioms.

9. Recasting
Explanation and Rationale
There is a fine line between giving students guidance which helps them to improve and providing a critique which leads to a loss of confidence. Most learners will involve their ego in what happens in the classroom. Depending on whether they perceive success or failure, they will react accordingly. Criticism, even if it is constructive, can often be taken by pupils to mean failure. Many of them do not have the means to disassociate themselves from the process of learning, nor have they the experience to take the long view (wherein difficulties are expected and accepted as a necessary part of achieving something distant). As a result, teachers need to be mindful of how the feedback they give may be interpreted.

With EAL learners the issue is especially acute. Developing their English language skills as they are, these students are likely to make more mistakes. That, of course, is part of learning. Because the peers who surround them are further along the language continuum, the errors of EAL learners can appear relatively greater. The difficulty for the teacher comes in wanting to praise and support EAL learners for the significant progress they are making, while also showing them how they might improve.

In terms of speaking, a sound method to follow is that of recasting. This praises students for the progress they make, provides a model of how to improve and avoids any suggestion of failure. It works as follows:

When speaking with EAL students, listen carefully to what they say. When you respond, comment positively (if appropriate) on the quality of what they have said. Then, recast their words so they are correct both grammatically and in terms of meaning. For example:

EAL Learner: *We went shops yesterday.*

Teacher: *Super answering of the question.* When you went to the shops yesterday, *what did you buy?*

No critique of the student's words in necessary. Modelling of the correct language is made into a part of the teacher's response. The EAL learner is given praise, and there is no risk of them losing confidence. Using this method consistently, throughout your verbal interactions with EAL learners, will lead to improvements in their speaking skills. They will be listening to you as a role model of good English usage; take this as an opportunity to recast their language into correct speech.

As your students grow in confidence, you may feel it appropriate to highlight your recasting of their words. You will need to assess how useful this explicit reference will be and what effects it might have on their confidence. If you feel happy that they have become sufficiently robust to deal positively with it, then you can proceed. The benefit of doing so is that you will be asking pupils to reflect on the differences between their own speech and your 'model' speech. In so doing, they will come to identify how they can close the gap. This will see them moving closer and closer to English usage which is both accurate and precise.

CHAPTER FIVE

Words, Reading, and Writing

We read for different reasons, and our expectations of texts differ accordingly; the standpoint from which one approaches a piece of writing influences what one is able to find or the interpretation one comes to make. In school, much of the reading we ask students to do is in pursuit of information. Some of this we expect them to absorb as knowledge. Other parts we hope will go toward developing their understanding.

We would do well to consider the context in which students meet texts and how this differs from our own experience of the texts. Take, for example, a geography textbook. For us, as adults and teachers, such a book has much with which we are familiar. This includes the geographical concepts and information, the layout (which is similar in general to textbook layouts and specifically to those used by geography textbooks), the pedagogical functions, and the use of a contents page and an index. For our students, the textbook is encountered for the first time. They see it as something which is being introduced to their world. We see it as something already a part of our world.

This is a fact easily forgotten. You or I might flick back and forth through a textbook with ease, skimming the pages for information we know is in there, for a purpose which we have identified long ago. This could be the planning of a lesson, for example, or the creating of a worksheet. Whatever it is, the chances are that we are using the text as a supplement to our own minds and doing so in a way which displays mastery.

A student who was using the same textbook would most likely find themselves faced with a mass of novel information presented in a structure which they would be able to follow, though perhaps not explain. A perceptive learner may be able to pick up on the reasons behind a certain layout or the rationale informing the choice of pictures, activities, and text. For many learners, however, such empathy is inaccessible. This is not least because of the great gulf between their life experience and that possessed by a person who writes such books. For us, as adults and teachers, the leap is not so great (if, indeed, there is any leap at all).

The point can be formulated as a general rule: try to conceive of the ways in which students will experience the texts you put in front of them.

In the case of EAL learners, your conception ought to be different again. These pupils will have the additional difficulty of decoding a language with which they may have little familiarity. Even if they are further along the language continuum, lots of texts used in lessons contain abstract, academic, and technical vocabulary. It is likely that many such words will be new to your EAL learners. Trying to conceive of how a situation like that might feel is the first step toward giving those students the kind of reading support from which they will benefit.

Moving away from the example of textbooks, we might point to the variety of texts which a student will be expected to read in a classroom. This includes writing on slides and worksheets, in the books of other students, on the walls (usually in the form of displays and rules), in planners, on registers, on doors (indicating, for example, the name of the teacher whose room it is), on computer screens, and in reference books such as dictionaries.

To skilled language users like you and me this range of written media gives little trouble. We would probably not even attend to the differences in structure and would instead group all the situations given above into a single, generic category: the written word in all its forms. We can do this because of our fluency and experience.

As well as being adept at understanding and using English orally and in writing, we are aware of the conventions surrounding the physical manifestation of words. So, for example, we understand what a register is and why it has names written in it. An EAL learner, who saw their name projected on a board as part of a list, with marks set down next to it, might be less sanguine. Without knowing the context of the writing which they are reading, they may be highly confused as to what is going on.

It is important to speak explicitly about the different texts a student might come across in the classroom. Ascertain through questioning whether or not EAL learners understand what the texts are for and the rules which govern their construction and use. If they do not, make it clear for them. This will help them to contextualise what they read. It could be within a framework of other texts and information or in relation to the role of such texts in the culture of the classroom.

For example, an EAL learner might join your class having come from a schooling system where indiscipline is dealt with quite differently to what you are used to. Let us say, hypothetically, that the student is unused to seeing rules written up and stuck on walls. It will be for you to describe the context in which these rules ought to be read. You will need to point out that:

- Rules play a major part in your classroom and the school.
- It is felt that everyone should be made aware of the rules.
- The rules are referred to when necessary. Hence it is useful to have a set close at hand.
- By having the rules clearly visible, it helps reinforce their power and the fact they are for everybody.
- Rule following is promoted by the visibility of the rules. This is seen as a good thing and, ultimately, encourages an internalisation of the positive behaviours which rule following promotes.

All of this is explicit. It needs to be brought out and made clear for EAL learners if they are to contextualise the rules on the wall as other students do. The same is true of other types of texts they will encounter in the classroom.

Taking our view from the general to the specific, we can think briefly about the different levels which exist in any one, single text. Three which are of particular importance are the levels of words, of sentences, and of meaning. These three levels operate independently but are also bound together.

To read successfully – that is, to look at words and to take knowledge and understanding away from them – we must first be able to identify the meaning of the majority of the words contained within a text. Some, perhaps, we can gloss over, working out what we think their meaning is from an analysis of their position in a sentence or their relationship to other words which we already know. However, we will need to be able to decode most of what we read; otherwise, the meaning each individual word is meant to convey will not be identified. It won't tally with what we have stored in our minds; those particular words will be unknown – nothing more than a collection of letters.

If we are at ease with the words themselves, then we need to be able to analyse how they have been placed in relation to one another. This we might refer to as the sentence level. Sentences are made up of groups of individual words. The meaning they convey comes from the words which go to make them up. The juxtaposition of words in a sentence also contributes to its meaning:

Hill up the go.
Go up the hill.

Being able to discriminate between sentences which convey meaning and those which do not is an indication of one's reading skills. So too is the understanding of how a sentence's meaning can be dependent on that which follows:

Go up the hill.
It was the last thing he ever said to me.
By the time I got back down the hill, he was gone.

In most pieces of text, a series of sentences are put together, each carrying meaning which is independent as well as contextual. By this we mean that any sentence could be taken out of the text, read on its own, and decoded for meaning, but that the specific meaning intended by the author comes also from that sentence's relationship to the sentences which surround it.

Following on from word and sentence levels is the more general level of meaning. This refers to the overall meaning – or meanings – of a text, the interpretation which the reader makes (this being close or not to the author's original intentions).

Let us look at an example. If a case reached the Supreme Court, the judges sitting there would need to make a ruling, usually on a particular point of law. This point would be dependent on the piece of text which either was the law or from which the law had come. Clearly, there would be a difference in them analysing the meaning of individual words in the text, analysing the meaning of specific sentences, and analysing the overall meaning, intended or imputed.

At the level of words, they may seek to clarify how a word such as 'intended' should be interpreted. At the level of sentences, they may need to specify what a sentence such as 'Any unlawful gain which may have been made through the action above mentioned ought to be confiscated' should be taken to mean. And, at the level of meaning, they would need to interpret the 'spirit of the law' and how it fits in with wider notions of jurisprudence.

Being aware of the different levels at which reading operates will help you to understand better the positions in which your EAL learners find themselves. It will make it easier for you to help them develop their abilities. It will also help you to avoid assumptions which might unwittingly stymie their progress or cause you to judge the efficacy of what you are doing incorrectly. Knowing, for example, that an ability to decode individual words does not *by necessity* lead to an ability to decode successive sentences dispels an assumption that, if held onto, could lead to much unnecessary consternation.

All texts which a student will read must first be written. An author needs to attend to the levels of word, sentence, and meaning if they are to communicate accurately that which they hope to convey. Even a set of classroom rules require these considerations. One must ask questions such as: Do any of the rules conflict with one another? Are the individual rules clear? Could any of the rules be taken to have a different interpretation? In addition, the wider meaning of the rules must be made clear. This is usually done through the writing of the rules in a list, perhaps a numbered list, with each one separated out to confer independent authority and importance. A title may signal what is to come beneath, and the colours and font chosen may accord with a particular purpose chosen by the writer. For example, a teacher who wishes to diminish the authoritarian element common to classroom rules may write them in Comic Sans MS. Doing this demonstrates an attention to the level of meaning.

When asking students to create written work, we will be expecting them to use the same process. It is good to talk to students about the different levels. Doing so gives them a set of analytical tools they can use to help make writing easier. EAL students may benefit from a discussion about how to analyse their own work. This will make it easier for them to identify whether or not they have achieved what they set out to do and how they might go about making improvements to their work.

Perhaps the greatest difficulty students encounter when writing is getting going and then keeping going. As stated in the introduction, writing is a technology. As such, its use has to be learnt, and practice is required before one becomes proficient. It sits in contrast to speech as an extension rather than a part of the human body. Students who are used to being able to communicate as and when they wish (by speaking) can easily become frustrated and demotivated when faced with the demands of writing.

Finding ways in which to sustain motivation and counteract some of the negative emotions writing can engender is a task common to all teachers. Students who are at an earlier stage of the language development continuum than their peers, including EAL students, are likely to be particularly vulnerable to these setbacks. Being alive to this gives the teacher a chance to preempt any problems. The way in which lessons are structured, the choice of activities, student groupings, and seating plans can all help avoid situations where learners feel put off by writing or incapable of doing what has been asked of them. The key is to set students up for success.

Linked to this point is the issue of what the writing you ask students to do is for. You might like to think about the reasons behind each piece of written work you set. Ask yourself what the primary goal of the work is. It could be:

- To give students an opportunity to communicate their thoughts on a topic.
- To provide the teacher with material which they can assess.
- To show knowledge and understanding (or lack thereof).
- To practise some aspect of writing.
- To work independently.
- To construct knowledge.
- To prepare for an activity.
- To engage actively with recently acquired knowledge.

Identifying the purpose behind written tasks will help ensure you are clear on what you are using them for. In turn, this will help you to help your students. Having something specific on which to focus is of far greater benefit than operating under a nebulous conception of 'doing some writing'.

I have sought to draw your attention to the fact that reading and writing are not as straightforward as might first appear and that this is especially true for EAL learners. What follows is a series of strategies, techniques, and activities which take account of these considerations.

1. Dictionaries

Explanation and Rationale

As humans we have a limited amount of memory. In the short term this is widely believed to be seven pieces of information, plus or minus two. The long-term memory is far more extensive, acting like a storehouse rather than a temporary depot. Some individuals are able to expand the scope of their memory through the use of techniques such as mnemonics or visualisation. With the addition of such strategies, the extent of what a person can recall increases significantly, comparing favourably to the abilities of the general population.

Memory techniques tend to have specific uses, some of which may be effective across the board. Their use is not a necessity, however, for individuals who seek to command a large amount of information with ease. There are other ways of doing that, and foremost among them is the use of reference books. If one knows there will not be a need to recall information at will (as in a memory contest), then reliance on books is quite acceptable, indeed preferable, given its ease and reliability.

Dictionaries are the most common form of reference book. They act as an extension of the human mind, providing a store of words and meanings which it would be difficult, perhaps impossible, to remember verbatim. As individuals age it is likely that they will internalise the spellings and meanings of more and more words. They may therefore rely less on dictionaries than a younger person. That said, they will still recognise their usefulness and remain safe in the knowledge that dictionaries are available to fall back on as and when required.

Encouraging EAL learners to use dictionaries is excellent for making them think carefully about words, for helping them to use and understand the English language, and for getting them into good habits for later life.

Example One

If an EAL learner is near the beginning of the language development continuum, ensure they have a bilingual dictionary for use in your classroom. These are readily available from physical and online booksellers and are relatively inexpensive. Such a dictionary will act as a bridge for students. It will connect together their existing knowledge (an understanding of their first language) with the new knowledge they are acquiring (an understanding of the English language).

The dictionary's use is twofold. First, it provides the pupil with a point of reference which they can continually return to as they are getting to grips with English. Second, it erases some of the sense of isolation which a student new to English might feel. Through the dictionary they can access meaning and spelling, starting from a position with which they are familiar (their first language). This breaks down the experience of alienation which can arise when one is first immersed in a new language. It provides a safe place to return to whenever one feels the need.

Example Two

Regularly model the use of dictionaries in front of students. When you introduce new words, or when you notice that an EAL learner has come across a word for the first time, make a show of getting hold of a dictionary and looking it up. Injecting some drama can help to enliven the experience. You might develop this by looking up new words with your students, before encouraging them to look new words up on their own. Have a collection of dictionaries in your room which are for pupils to use, and make it clear that that is what they are there for (sometimes dictionaries can become a piece of furniture, rather than a well-worn tool).

2. Sentence Starters

Explanation and Rationale

When trying to write, getting started can be the hardest thing. The blank page stares up from the desk offering no help and intimating that, among the seeming infinite supply of possibilities, you must decide what is to be done. And if you get it wrong, there will be no one but you to take the blame. It takes effort to go from nothing to something. Hauling oneself over the psychological barrier which forms between the writer and the empty page requires willpower. If one is confident, all is usually well. The writing flows because the mind feels certain in what it knows. But if this is not the case, there is work to be done.

Many students struggle to begin written work, including a great number of EAL learners. There are a number of reasons for this. First and foremost is a lack of confidence. This manifests itself in two ways: a belief from the student that they are not good at writing and will therefore make mistakes when they begin or a degree of indecision about how exactly they ought to start. The two points link together. In most cases it matters little how a piece of written work begins. There are better and worse ways, for sure, but no method, style, or set of words exists which are 'correct', to the exclusion of all others. Despite the cogency of this fact, it can be difficult for students to accept. If they see themselves as unconfident or as bad writers, then accepting it is asking for a major psychological shift, something which does not come easily to most people.

Sentence starters are a simple, effective means of getting round students' difficulties in beginning written work. They take the pressure off by signalling that an accepted way of starting exists. If the teacher is suggesting you begin like this, then it must be a good way to start (so the logic goes). Once students are up and running, they generally find continuing to write reasonably straightforward. Further difficulties may ensue, but these will be tempered by the fact that there is already writing on the page, providing evidence that the student can indeed 'do it'.

Example One

EAL learners, as well as encountering the issues noted above, may have trouble identifying and recalling the phrases and common collections of words that tend to be used to begin written work in the classroom. These include such examples as: 'In my opinion…'; 'Many people have said…'; 'I think that…' and so on. Assist them by putting up posters in your room with a range of sentence starters on them. Alternatively, print out and laminate a personal copy for each of your EAL learners.

Example Two

Include sentence starters on your resources. This could be done in one of two ways. First, include the starters on all your resources and indicate to the class that they are to be used by anybody who feels they would be helpful. Included in such a statement is the suggestion that EAL learners ought to use the sentence starters if they need to. Second, create differentiated materials for your EAL learners. These will carry similar content to that being studied by the rest of the class, as well as suitable sentence starters for the tasks you have set.

Example Three

Identify pieces of work produced by your students which include good, confident beginnings. Use this work as a model which the rest of you class, including EAL learners, can follow. Modelling can take one of three forms: (i) Place examples of the work on your classroom walls. Students are then allowed to go and look at it for inspiration. (ii) Spend time reading and discussing the exemplar student work. This could move from small group discussions to a whole-class consideration of why the work begins well and how others could learn from it. (iii) Create a bank of good starts by photocopying examples and collating them together in a book, on pieces of card, or on the wall. Encourage students to access these as they wish and to copy them if necessary.

3. Word Relationships

Explanation and Rationale

'Oh dear,' said the old dear, looking at the stuffed deer in the window.

'What's wrong, dearie?' said her friend, Deirdre.

'It's just very dear, my dear. I can't afford it after all.'

The words which go to make up any language possess a wide range of relationships. These may be the result of logic, history, or chance. In the example above we have a homophone (as in dear and deer), a homonym (as in the multiple usages of 'dear', each a different word despite the identical spelling and pronunciation), a suffix ('-ie' in dearie, a diminutive) and a word (Deirdre) which sounds similar to two others (deer and dear), yet appears to have no known link to these.

Paying attention to the relationships between words can help any learner develop a better understanding of the language they are studying. If one knows what the suffix '-ing' means, then one can make educated guesses about the relationship of new words ending in '-ing' to similar words which are already known. There may be cases where such guesses prove incorrect ('-ing' does not act as a suffix in the word 'thing') but we can learn from these, and there will be many cases where the application of knowledge proves correct.

Understanding relationships between words can provide shortcuts for language users. These include the opportunity to classify words. Coming to understand a relationship even as basic as the shared characteristics which all nouns possess can have a profound effect on how one uses and thinks about language.

For EAL learners, relationships which we take for granted may be difficult to spot, seemingly obtuse, or may even appear downright irrational. Such is the nature of language. It grows from the way in which people use it, not from some reasoned decision-making process. Being aware of this should cause one to be more attentive to word relationships when teaching, in order that they are demystified and made clear for EAL learners. The students will benefit considerably as a result.

Example One

Take opportunities to make connections for pupils between the roots of words. An example of this is the words 'muscle' and 'muscular'. By talking to students about such a connection, you can help them to group these words together in their minds. Another example would be 'write' and 'writing'. If you know there to be a number of words sharing a root, you could ask students to collect as many as they can. The lists they produce can be kept as reference tools until such a time as the student can do without them.

Example Two

Draw attention to homophones and homonyms. Homophones are words which are spelt differently but pronounced the same, for example, 'wood' and 'would'. Homonyms are words which are spelt and pronounced the same but have different meanings. For example, 'fox' (the animal) and 'fox' (to deceive or confuse someone). By making such relationships clear, you will help EAL learners to develop a better understanding of the varying meanings of words. This will in turn help them to avoid confusion when trying to decipher the meaning of other people's spoken and written words.

Example Three

Make a list of common suffixes and prefixes. This can then be placed on the wall of your classroom within clear view of EAL learners or given to them as a reference tool. Spend some time talking to students about the meaning of different suffixes and prefixes, what it is they *do* to the word to which they are attached. Find (or get students to find) simple examples of words containing the suffixes or the prefixes you have been looking at. Supplement these examples with pictures. A collection of illustrations, all showing people doing things (as in the example of '-ing' suffixed to verbs), for example, will quickly make clear to a student precisely what the relationship is between the words in question.

4. Word Taxonomies

Explanation and Rationale

Taxonomies are a means of dividing information into ordered groups or categories. They are a method of systematization in which similar things are collected together into different strata in a hierarchy. Each item within a particular taxonomy has two types of relationship. First, a relationship of similarity to the things with which it shares its group. Second, a relationship of difference, allied to either dominance or sub-jugation. A dominant difference exists between an item in the hierarchy and those things collected beneath it. A subjugated difference exists be-tween an item in the hierarchy and the things collected above it. Here are the top three levels of Bloom's taxonomy of educational objectives, which we can use as an example to illustrate these points:

Evaluation
(Assessing, judging, critiquing)
Synthesis
(Creating, uniting, planning)
Analysis
(Examining, investigating, testing)

'Uniting' has a relationship of similarity with 'creating' and 'planning'. They are all words which are examples of synthesis. It also has a relation-ship of dominant difference to all those words in the analysis category. And it has a relationship of subjugated difference to all those words in the evaluation category. In Bloom's taxonomy, evaluation is identified as a higher-level skill than synthesis, and this in turn is noted as a more difficult skill than analysis.

The word 'taxonomy' also refers to a subdiscipline of biological science. Taxonomists classify organic life-forms according to such criteria as species and genus. It is from this original discipline that the concept of taxonomy has migrated. This means that it can now be used to refer to the hierarchical classification of a wide range of different items.

Taxonomies have many benefits. Classifying items according to set criteria helps one develop a sense of where those items 'fit' in the overall structure. This notion of 'fit' is based on the relationships which individual items possess. Clearly, these relationships will be dependent on where the item is classified, and vice versa. The order which comes from such classification is conducive to developing understanding of the things contained therein.

Returning to Bloom's taxonomy, we can see that without the individual words being collected into more general categories, it would be far more difficult for a teacher to ascertain the relationships these words possess. Therefore, taxonomies store information about items.

This means they can aid EAL learners. Classifying words according to their relationships helps students to understand their meanings more easily. Here are two examples:

Classification of words in English language lessons according to their function: nouns, adjectives, verbs, and so on.

Classification of words in science lessons according to their size: smaller than a human, about the size of a human, larger than a human.

You will need to decide what categories are relevant for the topic you are teaching. Using taxonomies in this way may mean that sometimes there is no hierarchy. This is not a problem, as there is still a visible difference between items in one group and items in another group. For example, nouns are clearly different to verbs, despite not being in a relationship of dominance or subjugation.

You can create word taxonomies for your EAL learners, ask them to make them as they learn new words, or provide them with a structure (identifying different classes, for example) which they fill in as time goes by. Learners can use what they create as reference tools to help identify the correct use of words, both in terms speaking and in terms of writing.

5. Model Good Writing
Explanation and Rationale

The thought processes behind any piece of writing are often opaque. What one sees – reads – is the written response itself. While it is possible to infer or deduce some of what has led up to the decisions over language and meaning which the writer has taken, there will remain an element of doubt unless analysis is provided by the author. Even then, there is a possibility that the author will struggle to articulate why they wrote what they did. There may even be cases where the author cannot explain themselves at all. Perhaps they were *hit by inspiration* or *found their muse*. These two clichés signal the sometimes subconscious processes which seem to lead to breakthroughs, perhaps seen most commonly in creative writing.

When we pose questions for students, set them tasks, or ask them to respond to some stimulus material, we are expecting them to use specific processes. These include analysis of the question, ordering of information, testing of alternatives, logical sequencing, and so on. Each of these can be taken as a discrete process, although they tend to work in conjunction with one another. To some extent, it is expected that students will develop these skills – all of which are necessary precursors to good writing – through repetition coupled with feedback from teachers. Time and experience have shown this approach does work. However, it does so without attending explicitly to the things done before and during the act of writing.

EAL learners cannot call on years of practice writing in English. It will be to their benefit if the development of practical understanding can be speeded up. Modelling good writing is a means to do this. It involves the teacher creating their own written response to a question or task set for the class. The key difference is that the teacher should talk students through the process of writing, as they are doing it. This will demonstrate precisely what it is that a student ought to do in order to write well.

In addition, it will demystify the processes behind the creation of a written answer, giving clear guidance as to the separate things which any author needs to do. For example, you may explain how you go about analysing the question and the impact this has on how you structure your first few sentences. Further examples now follow.

Example One

Sit with an EAL learner, or a group of EAL learners, and demonstrate how to rewrite at the sentence level. Take a question or task and show them how you personally would construct a paragraph in response. Talk them through what you are thinking as you write. Once you have done this, read your paragraph aloud. Next, read it again, this time commenting on the strengths and weaknesses of what you have written in relation to the question. Make it clear what is good and what could be improved. More importantly, make it clear *why* certain things are good and why others need improvement.

Having done this, address the areas which need to be improved and explain how you will go about making the necessary improvements. Show students what the improvements will look like. And tell them what mental processes help you to achieve these results. The processes could include, for example, moving the subject of the sentence, synthesising the sentence so it says the same thing in fewer words, comparing the sentence to those around it and asking whether it fits, asking whether the sentence repeats information already given, and so on.

Example Two

Sit with an EAL learner, or a group of EAL learners, and demonstrate how you go about rewriting at the word level. Write a response, consisting of a few sentences, to a question or a task. As you write, explain how what you are doing relates to what the question or task has asked of you. Talk about the decisions you are making regarding what to write and in what order. When you have finished, read the sentences aloud. Then, read them again, this time identifying the strengths and weaknesses of the writing, paying particular attention to the choice of words.

Identify a range of words in your sentences that could be moved, removed, substituted, or altered (when you are writing, you may want to put things in which you know you will be able to pick up on here, so as to demonstrate a point). Talk to students about why you have selected particular words. Go through each one in turn and show how it could be changed. Explain why this would be an improvement and what caused you to make a change. For example, if you replace the word 'prior' with 'before' you may explain that 'before' is simpler than 'prior' and that they both convey the same meaning. Therefore, making the change retains the meaning of the sentence while making things clearer for the reader.

Example Three

Show EAL learners how to make the meaning of their writing precise by modelling dictionary use. Work with an individual or a group and pick out a question or task which asks for a written response. Talk to your learners about how you might plan an answer; draw out a range of different options and explain the criteria you would use to judge between them. Having decided upon your course of action, begin to write. Talk pupils through what you are doing at each stage. Remind them you chose a path before beginning and that you are now trying to stick to that path.

Have a dictionary to hand and refer to it regularly to check the meaning of the words you intend to use. Indicate to students how this checking involves comparing the meaning given by the dictionary with (i) the overall purpose you decided in advance and (ii) the specific intentions which led you to opt for certain words. If the meaning of the words does not accord with (i) and (ii), show students how to go about finding alternatives. Repeat this process until the writing is complete. Finish by rereading and comparing to your original plan.

6. Writing Frame

Explanation and Rationale

We have already noted that our short-term memory is limited. This can prove to be a hindrance when it comes to writing, particularly for those with little experience. Any piece of work over a paragraph in length requires the writer to conceive of both the individual item and the whole of which it is to become a part. A sentence is thus formed in the context of a paragraph, which itself is created in the context of a story, an essay, or some other overarching structure. For writing to be good, there must be coherence at all levels. The degree of this coherence can vary, but it must, at the least, be reasonably strong. If it is not, then the reader is likely to question why this is so. If the text provides no answer, then the reader will judge the writer – and the validity of what they have written – accordingly.

For writers such as our students, who have relatively limited experience with the written word, simultaneously attending to the immediate and the wider text is complicated by their need to think much more actively about the process of writing itself, including the very articulation of that which is in their minds; the synthesis of internal thought into written communication. An EAL learner who is anywhere other than at the far end of the language development continuum (close to mature native speakers) is unlikely to be adept at manipulating language.

It will take time and concerted effort for them to write their thoughts down in a manner which is clear and accurate. This is not to say they won't be able to do it, but the time and effort they exert will pull their minds away from considerations of coherency in relation to the text as a whole. Mastering the basics comes first. In practice, this means that extended writing is more difficult for EAL learners.

Writing frames can improve this situation. They provide students with a structure and remove many of the considerations regarding coherency that normally need to be considered. As with a number of the other strategies in this book, we have a tool that does some of the work for the student; a scaffold is created from which pupils can move off. It is akin to putting stabilisers on a bike. The support gives one a chance to get the basics right. On a bike with stabilisers the basics are balance and steering, in writing with a writing frame they are structure and coherency.

Example One

Provide students with a series of sentence starters covering each paragraph they will need to write. For example, the task is to write a weather report. The sentence starters could be: Welcome to the weather report…; The weather today has been…; Yesterday, the weather was…; We expect that tomorrow…; Our next report will be…

In this example we can see how the sentence starters make clear what the overall structure will be, as well as what each paragraph should contain. When adapting this model for your own use, you will need to take account of: what you are studying, the task or question in hand, and the point of language development your students are at.

Example Two

Outline how many paragraphs you would like students to write and what each paragraph should be about. For example, the question is, 'What is your life story?' To answer this question, you should write five paragraphs. Paragraph one: Who you are and where you come from.

Paragraph two: All about your family. Paragraph three: What things do you like, and what do you like to do in your spare time? Paragraph four: What do you want to do in the future? Paragraph five: What is your most memorable experience?

A writing frame like this lets students concentrate on writing each paragraph in turn. It breaks the question down into a series of simpler questions or tasks, the answers to which come together to create a whole. Pupils know that by dealing with each of the subquestions or tasks in turn, they will be answering the overall question.

Example Three

Introduce students to structures appropriate for different types of writing through generic writing frames. These types include things such as essays, reports, stories, experiment write-ups, newspaper articles, and so on. Here is an example for essay writing:

First paragraph: Introduction: In this essay I am going to…

Second paragraph: The first thing you think: My first point is that…

Third paragraph: The second thing you think: I also believe…

Fourth paragraph: A different point of view: Some other people might think…

Fifth paragraph: Conclusion: Overall, I think that…

The writing frame directs students as to what they must do in order to meet the demands of essay writing. There is a combination of what each part ought to entail, as well as an example of how one might go about beginning this. Type-specific writing frames can be used again and again. You can even print and laminate copies for EAL learners to keep for reference.

7. Prehighlight

Explanation and Rationale

When faced with a piece of unfamiliar text, there are various strategies which might be deployed. One might decide to read everything through and then to begin again, the idea being that the first run-through will help dispel unfamiliarity for the second reading. Another option is to look for elements with which one is familiar. These could be in the form of phrases, references, or specific words. By doing this, one is making connections to existing knowledge so as to remove some of the unfamiliarity. A third method would be to try to piece together the context surrounding the text: Who wrote it? Why did they write it? When was it published? Who was the intended audience? And so forth. Following this method may be somewhat time-consuming, although it is invariably worthwhile.

As teachers and adults we can make recourse to any of these approaches at will. We have lengthy experience of dealing with texts and have read a considerable amount through the course of our schooling and tertiary education. In addition, and in all probability, we will also have read a great deal in our leisure time and for the purposes of work.

Most students arrive at texts with far less information than we possess and with less understanding (if any at all) of the strategies available to help make the unfamiliar a little more recognisable. EAL learners are in a weaker position because they lack the context provided by earlier schooling and cultural experience (I am referring here to schooling in the English language and cultural experience in the English-speaking country in which they find themselves). This is in addition to their being at an earlier stage of English language development than their peers. Prehighlighting is a method the teacher can use to support EAL learners when they are dealing with texts.

Example One

If you are using photocopies of a text, make some extra copies for your EAL learners. Prior to the lesson, use a highlighter pen to draw attention to specific parts of the writing. These could be key words, important paragraphs, or some other thing to which you would like your learners to pay close attention. On handing out the sheets, indicate to your EAL learners that you would like them to concentrate on the parts you have highlighted. Tell them to ignore the rest of the text for the moment. This will help them to focus their efforts on manageable chunks of writing. It will also ensure they are attending to those parts which you have identified as being of greatest use (or, perhaps, those parts which are most accessible).

Example Two

Ask a student who is a skilled reader to go through a text you intend to use. Tell them their job is to identify all the key points and, once they have done this, to go through again and highlight these. You can set this task as an extension for able students and use the results with your EAL learners.

Example Three

If you do not have material which can be photocopied and find yourself working with textbooks instead, try using sticky notes instead of high-lighting. The end result will be the same. Of particular use are the sticky notes in the shape of arrows which you can buy at most stationers. Due to their shape, these can be used to point to sections on a page which you would like students to focus on. They can also be reused.

8. Purpose for Reading

Explanation and Rationale

Most reading is done for a purpose. It could be for pleasure, for learn-ing, or to find out information. If it is the first of these, then little is re-quired other than the selection of something which will bring pleasure. The last two entail something more. In both cases, things have to be done on top of the reading if one is to succeed.

Let us take reading for learning to begin. If you read a text with the intention of learning from it, then you must pay attention. If this is not done then the information conveyed through writing (and any accompa-nying tables, figures, and illustrations) will not pass into your own mind, at least, not in any usable form. There may be some imbibing of the text by a sort of osmosis, whereby you later remember or recognise snatch-es of what was written. However, to effectively assimilate information through reading – to learn it – attention must be paid.

If we wish to discover something by reading a text, then we need to analyse the material as we go. We must arrive at the writing with some notion of what we wish to find out and how we can go about discovering it. For example, if I want to know the current political situation in the Middle East, I might go to a broadsheet newspaper and look for articles in which the Middle East is mentioned. I would then analyse whether these articles contained information about the political situation there. They could, after all, be travel features. Upon ascertaining that some of the articles do contain the information I am looking for, I would need to analyse whether it is valid and reliable. This would involve asking ques-tions such as: Who wrote it? What are their credentials? How does the text compare to what I already know? What sort of language has been used? What reputation does the newspaper have?

In school we tend to ask students to read in order to learn and to find out information. Both processes require students to *do* things. Reading passively or inattentively is not sufficient. EAL learners will expend much effort trying to understand what they are reading on a basic level. They will also have to engage in the other processes we have mentioned. Here are some ways you can help them:

Example One

Write out a set of questions for your EAL learners. These should be analysis or comprehension questions. Pupils work through each one in turn, asking it of the text they are reading. This will help them to understand the piece of writing.

A good example of this approach comes from history. Here, students are encouraged to ask the same questions of any written source they study, questions such as: Who wrote it? Who was the audience? When was it written? How was it published? Is it corroborated by other sources?

Having a set of questions to refer to when reading helps to focus the reader's mind. It gives them a series of things to do, therefore providing structure and direction to the reading process.

Example Two

EAL learners may find it difficult to read a text, work out what it means, and analyse this meaning all at the same time. Reading frames can help to overcome this problem. Take a piece of A4 paper and divide it in three. In the top third, write: 'Words I do not know'. In the middle third, write: 'What is the writing about'. In the final third, write: 'What are the three key things in the writing?' Students can use the sheet as a guide to help them when reading. By working from top to bottom they will be going step-by-step from understanding, to meaning, to analysis. They fill in the sheet as they go along. This helps further by showing visually how the three processes – understanding the words, understanding the meaning, and analysing the whole – fit together. It emphasises their relationships and the fact that each relies on the former.

Example Three

Give EAL learners a piece of text to read. Ask them one simple question to which you would like to know the answer. Explain that the answer can be found by reading the text. Once they have managed this (and if they cannot, you might need to ask a simpler question, help them, or try a simpler text), ask them a slightly more difficult question, the answer to which is in the text. Repeat this process, ensuring the questions get progressively more difficult. In so doing, you will be helping learners to understand what analysing a text entails. They will be learning through doing. By pitching the questions right – moving gradually from simple to difficult – you will ensure students experience success. This will keep them motivated and guide them gently through increasingly complex thought processes.

9. Compare and Contrast
Explanation and Rationale

Meaning is based on difference. If something is one thing, it is that and nothing else. A cat is a cat in large part because it is not a dog, nor a hen, nor a pig, and so on. If a cat were close in nature to something else then we may question whether it ought to be seen as a thing in itself, or as part of that other group. In this way a lion and a tabby are both described as cats (albeit the former is often described as a 'big cat') and not as creatures sufficiently different to warrant separate identification.

The words we use to refer to things are arbitrary. A dog is a dog in English, yet it is a hund in German. That thing to which each word refers is the same. It does not possess some essence which leads to it being named in a certain way. Being referred to as 'dog' or 'hund' is not the result of something inherent to either an individual creature or to the species as a whole. Language, then, is a system of differences in which meanings are attached to specific words as well as being brought out by context (this covers the case of homonyms). In learning language we learn a system of differences. If a child cannot differentiate between the words 'mum' and 'dad' then it cannot communicate verbally or identify aurally the fact that language discriminates between what are, in the world as it were, mothers and fathers.

The identification of difference (and similarity) rests on the ability to compare and contrast. Consider the following snatch of conversation: 'Is it any good?' 'I don't know really; I need something to compare it with.' The second speaker, in order to answer the question, needs a reference point against which to compare the thing in question. It can only be good or not good in comparison to something. In this situation the thing in question is of a class not previously encountered by the respondent. They need more experience of these types of things in order to cast judgement over whether a particular item is good or not good.

EAL learners will have a limited experience of the English language. Therefore, they will have a limited stock of words on which to call for making comparisons. So too will they be limited in the range of sentences they can produce and therefore compare (sentences can carry meaning above and beyond that of the individual words through which they are composed). However, EAL learners will have experience of at least one other language. This can be harnessed for the purpose of making comparisons. And this can be of great benefit to students still developing their English language skills.

Example One

Provide your EAL learners with grids or frames in which they can record English words or sentences alongside equivalent words or phrases from their first language. This will allow students to make comparisons. It will give a clear display of the similarities and differences; words and sentences carrying the same meanings, yet from different languages, are set against one another.

Example Two

This strategy develops out of the use of grids or frames. Once students have filled in one or more of these, ask them to look for patterns or surprises. For example, it may be that the personal pronoun 'I' is placed at a similar point in a sentence in English as the equivalent word in the learner's first language. Another example may be that in English only proper nouns are capitalised, whereas in some other languages the conventions are different. The purpose of this strategy is to encourage students to make comparisons and contrasts between their first language and English. By doing this, they will develop a better understanding of the latter. It will also help them to realise that knowledge of a first language can be of great benefit when learning a second (or third, or fourth) – a fact that may not be readily apparent.

Example Three

Ask students to answer questions in English and in their first language. Next, talk through their answers with them. Ask the pupils to make comparisons, to identify differences, and to pick out similarities. Use students' findings to stimulate a discussion. Ensuing conversations will help learners to think carefully about the structure of English, the meanings of specific words, and the rules which guide sentence and paragraph construction.

10. Plan in First Language
Explanation and Rationale

When we set students the task of producing a piece of writing, whatever that piece of writing is to entail, we are making a series of demands of them, two of which are of central importance. First, we are asking them to conceive of a response to whatever it is that we have set – answering a question, responding to a stimulus, completing an assignment. This will involve them thinking about the task. They will have to consider various ways by which they might respond and how these different approaches might play out in terms of an end result. Second, we are asking students to put their ideas into words.

The key skill, one might say, is to bridge the gap between the conception and the execution. The closer the written work is to what the student intended, the more accurately they are conveying their thoughts. Looked at in this way, we can see how important a mastery of writing is if you want others to understand what you think.

Achieving mastery is difficult. This is exacerbated for EAL learners because they will most likely be at an early stage of the language development continuum. Therefore, they have a weaker grasp of the English language, including its written component. The process of turning thoughts into writing is thus all the harder. Students have to attend closely to the language as a thing in itself, as well as an attempted manifestation of what is in their minds.

Encouraging students to plan in their first language mitigates this problem, to some extent. Students will be able to fix and formalise their thoughts in their first language and then use this as a guide. They can translate or recreate what they have written, not having to pay as much attention to the pairing up of words and thoughts. This allows them to concentrate on using English correctly and writing in a manner which is accurate.

Example One

Give your EAL learners a rough book. Tell them they should use this to plan their written work in their first language before going on to write in English. Explain the reasoning behind the method and press home the fact that they will have skill and mastery in their first language and can put this to good use (in some instances this may not be the case. However, such situations are likely to be in the minority). You might develop this technique by asking students to talk you through some of the planning they do in their rough book. This will help build rapport – you are showing an interest in the student's own language even though you may struggle to understand it – and encourage your students to think and talk about the processes they have used to translate their thoughts into writing.

Example Two

This links to another strategy mentioned elsewhere. Give EAL learners a mini-whiteboard, marker pen, and board wipe. Ask them to use this before writing in English. Tell them to organise their ideas in their first language. Explain they could plan a sentence at a time, paragraph by paragraph, or they could plan their whole piece before starting; make sure they know it is up to them. The mini-whiteboard will act as a thinking space for students – an extension of their mind, if you will. It can do the job of holding meaning and structure while pupils concentrate on getting the correct English words and putting them together in the right order.

Example Three

Give students a piece of A4 paper with a line drawn down the middle. Explain that one half of the paper is for writing in English and the other half is for writing in their first language. Ask students to respond to your task in their first language before writing anything in English. Indicate that by separating their points or paragraphs they will be making a series of entries which they can then marry up with English-language counterparts. Their finished sheet will look a little like an entry in a translation book. Working in this way helps EAL learners to split up the processes involved in writing in English. This makes their job easier, as they only have to deal with one process at a time.

CHAPTER SIX

Conclusion

If there is one thing I would urge you to take away from this book, it is this: think carefully about language. Doing so will ensure that your EAL learners succeed and flourish in your lessons. It can be easy for us, as skilled, mature language users, to lose sight of the challenges facing a student who is still developing their understanding of English. We must try to place ourselves in their shoes and empathise with their situation. At the same time, though, we need to retain our own perspective – that of the teacher – and the analytical capacities which go with it. In so doing we can identify the difficulties students will face and then use our own skills to find ways in which to help them overcome these.

It will no doubt be clear that this approach, and indeed most of what is included in this book, is not so much good EAL teaching as just good teaching. This ought to be the case if we are to stand by the premise, outlined in the introduction, that EAL learners should be seen as similar to other students, with differences stemming from their relative inexperience with English. This led us to advocate a model of a language development continuum, upon which all students can be placed. Those learners designated as EAL would be nearer the start of this continuum and likely to progress along it at different rates until such a time as they have closed the gap on their peers.

What has been implicit throughout is that students who are not learning English as an additional language will occupy a range of different positions on the continuum. Some native speakers may in fact share in the difficulties which EAL learners encounter. It is not uncommon, for example, for students to reach the next stage of their schooling with significantly lower reading ages than those of their contemporaries. They will benefit from many of the strategies outlined in this book, just as EAL learners will.

What is being put forward then is a general approach to teaching in which the language needs of all learners are carefully considered and in which EAL students are given more attention. The teacher is encouraged to look at all aspects of their own practice and the physical space in which they work in order to find ways in which they can aid help students to develop their language skills. This includes the basic point of doing as much as possible to make communication between teacher and students as clear and as accurate as it can be. The teacher should always remember their position as a model language user. They will be teaching students not just through the lessons they plan but also through the way in which they speak and act.

I have broken the strategies, activities, and techniques down into four sections: Speaking and Listening; Images; The Teacher; and Words, Reading, and Writing. While it has been useful to use the four categories as a means of delineating the ideas in the book and analysing some different aspects of language and communication, it is also important to remember that, despite their differences, they share many of the same roots. When working with language learners in the classroom, one should always be seeking to interweave ideas from the different categories in order to create a cumulative effect.

Another point to note is that there are a lot of different strategies, techniques, and activities contained in the book. For most of the entries there are three examples, further extending the range of options available to you. I have found from my own experience that it is best to focus on a small range of activities at first, in order to master them, before broadening out and enlarging one's repertoire. I would advise following such an approach when putting the ideas in this book into practice.

Teaching has a large element of trial and error to it. What works with one student may fail miserably with another. What delights one class may elicit derision from a different set of students. What advances learning rapidly in one setting may stall it in a different situation. Retaining your principles while you adapt and edit your approach is important. It provides continuity and philosophical consistency amid the changes you make. This helps ensure those changes are underpinned by the purposes you had in mind in the first place. These can easily be lost under the pressure induced by a difficult lesson.

The principles put forth in this book:

- That language ought to be given serious consideration.
- That EAL learners are largely similar to other learners.
- That language development is a continuum upon which we can all be placed and along which we can all make progress.

These principles underpin everything which has been written. This in itself should serve as an example of the coherency and sustained purpose which can be maintained through a range of disparate situations. It is harder in the classroom, I know. Especially when learners are making demands of you and your time is severely circumscribed. Nonetheless, take on board the principles which have been set out here and keep them at the forefront of your mind when working with your students.

By doing this you will be drawing together theory and practice. You will be modelling the kind of rationality which we want all our pupils to develop: that of using reasoning, experience, and evidence in order to make carefully considered decisions. But, also, you will be giving your students, and in particular your EAL students, the best possible chance to succeed. You will be creating environments for them in which their learning is supported and their needs are used to inform the planning which you do. Of course, if something arises that makes you question the principles, then you will need to follow that path as well. However, until it does, keep these guiding lights in mind and, where appropriate, share them with your students.

Bibliography

Black, Paul, Wiliam, Dylan, et al., *Assessment for Learning: Putting It Into Practice*. Maidenhead: Open University Press, 2003

Bruner, J., *Acts of Meaning*. Cambridge, Massachusetts: Harvard University Press, 1990

Bruner, J., *Child's Talk: Learning to Use Language*. New York: WW Norton & Co., 1983

Bruner, J., *The Culture of Education*. Cambridge, Massachusetts: Harvard University Press, 1996

Cummins, J., *Language, Power and Pedagogy*. Clevedon: Multilingual Matters, 2000.

Dewey, J., *Experience and Education* (Reprint edition). New York: Touchstone, 1997 [1938]

Donaldson, M., *Children's Minds*. London: Fontana, 1978

Mercer, N., *The Guided Construction of Knowledge: Talk Amongst Teachers and Learners*. Clevedon: Multilingual Matters, 1995

Mercer, N., *Words and Minds: How We Use Language to Think Together*. London: Routledge, 2000

Petty, Geoff, *Teaching Today: A Practical Guide*. Cheltenham: Nelson Thornes, 2004

Pim, Chris, *How to Support Children Learning English as an Additional Language*. Hyde: LDA, 2010

Vygotsky, L., *Mind and Society* (M. Cole, V. John-Steiner, S. Scribner, and E. Souberman, Eds.). Cambridge, Massachusetts: Harvard University Press, 1978

Vygotsky, L., *Thought and Language* (Revised and edited by Alex Kozulin). Cambridge, Massachusetts: Massachusetts Institute of Technology, 1986

Washbourne, Alice, *EAL Pocketbook.* Alfresford: Teachers' Pocketbooks, 2011